AMERICA'S HOMELAND WARRIORS

AMERICA'S POLICE OFFICERS AND THE WAR ON TERROR

BY
LIEUTENANT STEVEN L. ROGERS

Airleaf Publishing

airleaf.com

ISBN: 1-59453-905-7

TABLE OF CONTENTS

CHAPTER 1
INTRODUCTION

In January 2000, several American police officials visited the Israeli police in Jerusalem to learn how to deal with terrorist attacks as well as how to address public reaction to them.

During a 2000 news interview, Van A. Harp, the head of the FBI's Washington Field Office said that the reason why police officials went to Israel to learn how to deal with terrorist activity was because Israel is the "epicenter of terrorism."

Hundreds of Israeli citizens have died in dozens of terrorist incidents that occurred during the past two decades. Yet the citizens of Israel live a normal life. Israeli Police say that their citizens continue to move forward and overcome the fear of attacks because they feel they are a part of the war against terror.

"It's a partnership between the police and the people that keep us alive. Policing in our nation has changed forever. It will never be like the old days," says a top Israeli police official.

Like Israel, America's police officers and the citizens they are called to protect and serve are going to meet the most difficult challenges in the history of the republic as this century moves forward. Indeed, policing in America is changing forever.

On September 11th 2001, the mission of police departments across America changed from "routine" crime fighting to specific mission oriented policing designed to defeat an enemy never before seen within the borders of our nation. On that horrific September morning, America's homeland was viciously attacked like at no other time in history. The scenes of two giant airliners ripping through the World Trade Center in New York City, an airliner crashing into the Pentagon in Northern Virginia, and a jet smashing into the ground in western Pennsylvania, will forever be etched in the minds of the people who lived to witness this day of infamy.

Also etched in the minds of the American people who lived to see that day are the brave fireman, police officers, rescue workers and ordinary citizens who ran into harms way to save the lives of many of their fellow citizens. The world witnessed the first American "army" to enter what was the beginning of a war against an evil and formidable enemy whose objective was then and still is today, to destroy the United States of America.

Unlike fighting the "common criminal" who commits his or her criminal act for personal satisfaction or financial gain, the enemy we now face is a well trained ruthless warrior whose objective is to rein terror on our streets, kill our people, and destroy our way of life.

Police departments in the United States are the most technologically advanced law enforcement organizations in the world. American police departments are well prepared to bring criminals to justice and to prevent crime from flourishing in our cities. However, the enemies we will be facing in this new century are not the traditional criminal types. Instead, they are "criminal-warrior types" never before seen in our nation. This brand of criminal roaming our land and plotting to destroy us isn't satisfied with a break-in, a robbery, or an assault. This "criminal-warrior" is satisfied with one thing only-death and destruction.

Police officers and citizens from every city and town across America are facing their greatest challenges. These challenges will require police administrators to shift priorities from traditional crime fighting methodologies to a new kind of urban warfare. All the high-tech equipment police departments have installed in patrol cars and headquarters buildings throughout our nation are no match for the guerilla war about to come to the streets of America.

This book will give every police officer and citizen a basic understanding about the enemy seeking to destroy us, the challenges law enforcement is facing, and how, by working together, we can prevent a rein of terror from sweeping across our nation.

As we enter this new century, with this new challenge, against a new enemy, let us keep in mind the words of Abe Lincoln who met the challenges of his time: *"The dogmas of the past are inadequate to the stormy present. The occasion is piled high with difficulty, and we must rise with the occasion. As our case is new, we must think anew, and act anew."*

CHAPTER 2
THE ROOTS OF AMERICA'S PROBLEM

There is a history with regard to America's present day problems that involve the Middle East. This history has roots that go back to the late 19th and early 20th Century.

However, it is the events that unfolded in the late 20th Century that gave birth to the problems we are facing today, especially the problems related to Islamic radicalism, Iran, and Iraq.

Our troubles with Iran began in 1953, when the U.S. allegedly supported a coup of the Iranian government, replacing a popular leader with what the Iranian public viewed as an American puppet- Mohammad Reza Shah Pahlavi.

Under the leadership of Shah Pahlavi, the government of Iran became a ruthless regime. Anyone who opposed his leadership was imprisoned, tortured, and sentenced to death. The people of Iran knew that the Shah was supported by the U.S. and therefore placed full responsibility for his actions at the doorstep of the White House.

During the late 1950's through the 1980's the U.S. government needed the Shah to help contain the Soviet Union. Hence, U.S. government officials were not about to interfere with Iran's internal affairs. However, in the eyes of the Iranian people, the U.S. government had already interfered in Iran's internal affairs by getting involved in the 1953 coup, which set the stage for the introduction of Islamic radicalism and their chief leader, Ayatollah Khomeini.

In 1964, Khomeini was sent into exile, eventually ending up in Iraq. From Iraq, he launched a series of vicious verbal attacks on the monarchy, first against the Shah who exiled him and later against the Shah's son who succeeded him to the throne.

Khomeini was a Shi'ite Muslim, but his beliefs were an extreme form of the Shi'a creed. From exile, he developed the concept of a theocracy, which dramatically changed what had previously been a largely apolitical branch of Islam.

Khomeini accused the Shah of supporting Israel and the U.S. claiming that he (the Shah) was an American agent working to westernize Iran. Throughout the 60s and 70s Khomeini built a power base of support in Iran and organized demonstrations that lead to the downfall of the Shah, thus ushering him into power.

In 1979, Ayatollah Khomeini became the undisputed religious leader and dictator of Iran. Once in power, he isolated his government from most of the world, and embraced only those who supported his vision for a strong Islam. He became the Supreme Ruler of Iran and in effect became a dictator. He instituted Islamic law and suspended secular law with religious law.

In 1979, he led the taking over the U.S. Embassy and taking of U.S. hostages, which lasted for over a year. They were released after the defeat of President Carter and the inauguration of Ronald Regan.

In 1980, Iraq invaded Iran. The Soviets aided Iran while the U.S. aided Iraq. The war lasted for eight years with no clear victor. It was soon after this war that Khomeini began to support international terrorism.

In the eyes of the Iranian people, Khomeini was a hero for standing up to the "Great Satan", the United States. To this day, the people of Iran have very deep-seated unjustified anger at the U.S. Hence, their government's support of Islamic terrorism.

When the Soviets invaded Afghanistan in 1979, the Afghan forces were taking a beating. The concern of the U.S. was that if the Soviets won, they would have a military presence in the Mid-East and perhaps disrupt the balance of power in the region. However, the Afghan rebels were eventually able to neutralize the Soviet military through the use of modern weapons supplied by the United States government. What is ironic is that Usama Bin Laden was an Afghan fighter during this time. Therefore, the United States was unknowingly supporting a future enemy.

In 1988, the United States, Pakistan, Afghanistan, and the Soviet Union signed an agreement for the withdrawal of Soviet troops and the return of Afghanistan to nonaligned status.

In 1992, Islamic radicals created a new transitional government and Afghanistan became an Islamic republic, which supported, financed, and trained terrorists from throughout the world.

It is important to note that after the Soviet-Afghan war, the Islamic radicals actually believed that when they fought off the Soviets, the U.S. had nothing to do with their victory. The Afghan fighters were trained by the U.S. in covert and overt ops, in intelligence gathering, and in specific types of warfare to defeat the Soviets. However, they were convinced that they could stare down any nation, no matter how powerful, including the United States.

Early after the war, Bin Laden began to plan his moves against America. He knew he could never beat the U.S. in a conventional war. However, he concluded that the only way to bring America to its knees was to launch a devastating, demoralizing blow, designed to sap the will and strength of the U.S. With quiet support from Iran, Iraq, and other mid-east countries, Usama Bin Laden launched the war against America in 2001.

The next chapter contains "the tree" and "branches" which came from the "roots" you just read about. The "tree" is the Al Qaida Training Manual which was written by Bin Laden. The "branches" are the specific instructions he included in the manual. This is a must read for every police officer in America. Knowledge is power! And in the case of terrorism, the more power we have over our enemy, the better chance we have to survive from his deadly acts.

CHAPTER 3
THE TREE AND ITS BRANCHES

AL QAIDA TRAINING MANUAL

While reading this chapter, pay special attention to the sections which relate to use of apartments, tourist attractions, etc.

PRINCIPLES OF MILITARY ORGANIZATION

Military Organization has three main principles without which it cannot be established.

1. Military Organization commander and advisory council.
2. The soldiers (individual members).
3. A clearly defined strategy.

Military Organization Requirements: The Military Organization dictates a number of requirements to assist it in confrontation and endurance. These are:

1. Forged documents and counterfeit currency.
2. Apartments and hiding places.
3. Communication means.
4. Transportation means.
5. Information.
6. Arms and ammunition.

7. Transport.

<u>Missions Required of the Military Organization:</u>

The main mission for which the Military Organization is responsible is:

The overthrow of the godless regimes and their replacement with an Islamic regime.

Other missions consist of the following:

1. Gathering information about the enemy, the land, the installations, and the neighbors.
2. Kidnapping enemy personnel as well as foreign tourists.
3. Assassinating enemy personnel as well as foreign tourists.
4. Freeing brothers who are captured by the enemy.
5. Spreading rumors and writing statements that instigate people against the enemy.
6. Blasting and destroying the places of amusement, immorality, and sin; not a vital target.
7. Blasting and destroying the embassies and attacking vital economic centers.
8. Blasting and destroying bridges leading into and out of the cities.

IMPORTANCE OF THE MILITARY ORGANIZATION

1. Removal of those personalities that block the call's path. All type of military and civilian intellectuals for the State.

2. Proper utilization of the individuals' unused capabilities.
3. Precision in performing tasks, and using collective views on completing a job from all aspects, not just one.
4. Controlling the work and not fragmenting it or deviating from it.
5. Achieving long-term goals such as the establishment of an Islamic state and short-term goals such as operations against enemy individuals and sectors.
6. Achieving the conditions for possible confrontation with the regressive regimes and their persistence.
7. Achieving discipline in secrecy and through tasks.

SECOND LESSON: NECESSARY QUALIFICATIONS AND CHARACTERISTICS FOR THE ORGANIZATION'S MEMBERS

1. ISLAM: The member of the Organization must be Moslem. How can an unbeliever, someone from a revealed religion, a secular person, a communist, etc. protect Islam and Moslems and defend their goals and secrets when he does not believe in that religion?

The Israeli Army requires that a fighter be of the Jewish religion. Likewise, the command leadership in the Afghan and Russian armies requires any one with an officer's position to be a member of the communist party.

2. COMMITMENT TO THE ORGANIZATION'S IDEALOGY: This commitment frees the Organization members from conceptual problems.

3. MATURITY: The requirements of military work are numerous, and a minor cannot perform them. The nature of hard and continuous work in dangerous conditions requires a great deal of psychological, mental, and intellectual fitness, which are not usually found in a minor. It is reported that Ibn Omar - may Allah be pleased with him - said, 'During Ahad [battle] when I was fourteen years of age, I was submitted to the prophet - GBAKH. He refused me and did not throw me in the battle. During Khandak [trench] Day [battle] when I was fifteen years of age, I was also submitted to him, and he permitted me.'

4. SACRIFICE: He has to be willing to do the work and undergo martyrdom for the purpose of achieving the goal and establishing the religion of majestic Allah on earth.

5. LISTENING AND OBEDIENCE: In the military, this is known today as discipline. It is expressed by how the member obeys the orders given to him. That is what our religion urges. The Glorious says 'O ye who believe! Obey Allah and obey the messenger and those charged with authority over you.' In the story of Hazifa Ben Al-Yaman - MAHMOH - who was exemplary in his obedience to Allah's messenger - ABAKH - sent him to spy on the Kureish and their allies during their

siege of Madina, Hazifa said "As Mohammed called me by name to stand he said 'Go get me information about those people and do not alarm them about me.

6. KEEPING SECRETS AND CONCEALING INFORMATION: [secrecy is important] Even with the closest people, for deceiving enemies is not easy. Allah says "Even though their plots were such that as to shake the hills!" Allah's messenger - GBAKH - says, 'Seek Allah's help in doing your affairs in secrecy. It was in the proverbs 'The hearts of freemen are the tombs of secrets' and 'Moslems' secrecy is faithfulness, and talking about it is faithlessness.' [Mohammed] - GBAKH - used to keep work secrets from the closest people, even from his wife A'isha - MAGBOH.

7. FREE OF ILLNESS: The Military Organization's member must fulfill this important requirement. Allah says, 'There is no blame for those who are infirm, or ill, or who have no resources to spend.

8. PATIENCE: [member] should have plenty of patience for afflictions if he is overcome by the enemies. He should not abandon this great path and sell himself and his religion to the enemies for his freedom. He should be patient in performing the work, even if it lasts a long time.

9. TRANQUILITY AND UNFLAPPABILITY: [he] should have a calm personality that allows him to endure psychological traumas as those involving

bloodshed, murder, arrest, imprisonment, and reverse psychological traumas such as killing one or all of his Organization's comrades. [he should] carry out the work.

<u>10. INTELLIGENCE AND INSIGHT</u>: When the prophet - ABKH - sent Hafiza Ben Al-Yaman to spy on the polytheist and Hafiza sat among them, Abou Soufian said 'Let each of you look at his companion.'

In World War I, the German spy, Julius Seelber [PH] managed to enter Britain and work as a mail examiner due to the many languages he had mastered. From the letters, he succeeded in obtaining important information and sent it to the Germans. One of the letters that he checked was from a lady who had written to her brother's friend in the fleet. She mentioned that her brother used to live with her until he was transferred to a secret project that involved commercial ships. When Seelber read that letter, he went to meet that young woman and blamed her for her loose tongue in talking about military secrets. He skillfully managed to draw out of her that her brother worked in a secret project for arming old commercial ships. These ships were to be used as decoys in the submarine war in such a way that they could close to the submarines, as they appeared innocent. Suddenly, cannonballs would be fired from the ship's hidden cannons on top of the ships, which would destroy the submarines. 48 hours later that secret was handed to the Germans.

11. CAUTION AND PRUDENCE:
A: In his battle against the king of Tomedia, the Roman general Speek sent an emissary to discuss with that king the matter of truce between the two armies. In reality, he had sent him to learn about the Tomedians' ability to fight. The general picked Lilius, one of his top commanders, for that task and sent with him some of his officers, disguised as slaves. During that mission, one of the king's officers, Sifax, pointed to one of the slaves and yelled, 'That slave is a Roman officer I had met in a neighboring city. He was wearing a Roman uniform.' At that point, Lilius used a clever trick and managed to divert the attention of the Tomedians from that by turning to the disguised officer and quickly slapping him on the face a number of times. He reprimanded him for wearing a Roman officer's uniform when he was a slave and for claiming a status he did not deserve. The officer accepted the slaps quietly. He bowed his head in humility and shame, as slaves do. Thus, Sifax's men thought that officer was really a slave because they could not imagine that a Roman officer would accept these hits without defending himself.

King Sifax prepared a big feast for Lilius and his entourage and placed them in a house far away from his camp so they could not learn about his fortifications. They [the Romans] made another clever trick on top of the first one. They freed one of their horses and started chasing him in and around the camp. After they learned about the extent of the fortifications they caught the horse and, as planned, managed to abort their mission about the truce agreement. Shortly after their return, the Roman general attacked King Sifax' camp and burned the fortifications. Sifax was forced to seek reconciliation.

B. There was a secret agent who disguised himself as an American fur merchant. As the agent was playing cards aboard a boat with some passengers, one of the players asked him about his profession. He replied that he was a 'fur merchant.' The women showed interest and began asking the agent many questions about the types and prices of fur. He mentioned fur price figures that amazed the women. They started avoiding and regarding him with suspicion, as though he were a thief or crazy.

12. TRUTHFULNESS AND COUNSEL: The Commander of the faithful, Omar Ibn-Khattab - MABAKH - asserted that this characteristic was vital in those who gather information and work as spies against the Moslems' enemies. He sent a letter to Saad Ibn Abou Wakkas - MABPWH - saying, 'If you step foot on your enemies' land, get spies on them. Choose those whom you count on for their truthfulness and advice, whether Arabs or inhabitants of that land. Liars' accounts would not benefit you, even if some of them were true; the deceiver is a spy against you and not for you.

13. ABILITY TO OBSERVE AND ANALYZE: The Israeli Mossad received news that some Palestinians were going to attack an Israeli El Al airplane. That plane was going to Rome with Golda Meir - ACUH - the Prime Minister at the time, on board.

The Palestinians had managed to use a clever trick that allowed them to wait for the arrival of the plane without being questioned by anyone. They had beaten a man who sold potatoes, kidnapped him, and hidden him. They made two holes in the top of that peddler's cart and placed two tubes next to the chimney through which two Russian-made 'Strella' missiles could be launched. The Mossad officers traveled the airport back and forth looking for the Palestinians. One officer passed the potato cart twice without noticing anything. On his third time, he noticed three chimneys, but only one of them was working with smoke coming out of it. He quickly steered toward the cart and hit it hard. The cart overturned and the Palestinians were captured.

14. ABILITY TO ACT, CHANGE POSITIONS, AND CONCEAL ONESELF

a. Noaim Ibn Mosoud had done in his mission to cause agitation among the tribes of Koraish, those of Ghatfan, and the Jews of Korethia. He would control his reactions and managed to skillfully play his role. Without showing signs of inconsistency, he would show his interest and zeal towards the Jews one time and show his concern about the Koraish at another.

b. In 1960, a car driven by an American colonel collided with a truck. The colonel lost consciousness, and while unconscious at the hospital, he started speaking Russian fluently. It was later discovered that the colonel was a Soviet spy who was planted in the United States. He had fought in Korea in order to conceal his true identity and to gather information and critical secrets. If not for the collision, no one would have suspected or confronted him.

THIRD LESSON: COUNTERFEIT CURRENCY AND FORGED DOCUMENTS Financial Security Precautions:

1. Dividing operation funds into two parts: One part is to be invested in projects that offer financial return, and the other is to be saved and not spent except during operations.
2. Not placing operation funds in one place.
3. Not telling the Organization members about the location of the funds.
4. Having proper protection while carrying large amounts of money.
5. Leaving the money with non-members and spending it as needed.

Forged Documents (ID cars, record books, passports): The following security precautions should be taken:

1. Keeping the passport in a safe house so it would not be seized by the security apparatus, and the brother

it belongs to would have to negotiate its return (I'll give you your passport if you give me information.)

2. All documents of the undercover brother should be falsified.
3. When the undercover brother is traveling with a certain identity card or passport, he should know all pertinent information such as the name, profession, and place of residence.
4. The brother who has special work status (commander, communication link, etc) should have more than one identity card and passport. He should learn the contents of each, the nature of the profession, and the dialect of the residence area listed in the document.
5. The photograph of the brother in these documents should be without a beard. It is preferable that the brother's public photograph be also without a beard. If he already has one showing a photograph with a beard, he should replace it.
6. When using an identity document in different names, no more than one such document should be carried at one time.
7. The validity of the falsified travel documents should always be confirmed. All falsification matters should be carried out through the command and not haphazardly (procedural control).
8. Married brothers should not add their wives to their passports.
9. When a brother is carrying the forged passport of a certain country, he should not travel to that country. It is easy to detect forgery at the airport, and the

dialect of the brother is different from that of the people from that country.

10. Security Precautions Related to the Organizations' Given Names: The name of the Organization should not be odd in comparison with other names around him.
11. A brother should not have more than one name in the area where he lives (the undercover work place.)

FOURTH LESSON: ORGANIZATION MILITARY BASES APARTMENT PLACES & HIDING

Definition of Bases: These are apartments, hiding places, command centers, etc. in which secret operations are executed against the enemy. These bases may be in cities, and are called homes or apartments. They may be in mountainous, harsh terrain far from the enemy, and are called hiding places or bases. During the initial stages, the Military Organization usually uses apartments in cities as places for launching assigned missions, such as collecting information, observing members of the ruling regime, etc.

Hiding places and bases in mountains and harsh terrain are used at later stages, from which Jihad groups are dispatched to execute assassination operations of enemy individuals, bomb their centers and capture their weapons. In some Arab countries such as Egypt, where there are no mountains or harsh terrain, stages of Jihad work would take place in cities. The opposite was true in Afghanistan, where initially Jihad work was in the cities, and then the warriors shifted to mountains and harsh terrain. There, they started battling the Communists.

<u>Security Precautions Related to Apartments</u>

1. Choosing the apartment carefully as far as the location, the size for the work necessary (meetings, storage, arms, fugitives, work preparation).
2. It is preferable to rent apartments on the ground floor to facilitate escape and digging of trenches.
3. Preparing secret locations in the apartment for securing documents, records, arms, and other important items.
4. Preparing ways of vacating the apartment in case of surprise attack (stands, wooden ladders).
5. Under no circumstances should any one know about the apartment except those who use it.
6. Providing the necessary cover for the people who frequent the apartment (students, workers, employees, etc.)
7. Avoiding seclusion and isolation from the population and refraining from going to the apartment at suspicious times.
8. It is preferable to rent these apartments using false names, appropriate cover, and non-Moslem appearance.
9. A single brother should not rent more than one apartment in the same area, from the same agent, or using the same rental office.
10. Care should be exercised not to rent apartments that are known to the security apparatus [such as] those used for immoral or prior Jihad activities.

11. Avoiding police stations and government buildings. Apartments should not be rented near those places.
12. When renting these apartments, one should avoid isolated or deserted locations so the enemy would not be able to catch those living there easily.
13. It is preferable to rent apartments in newly developed areas where people do not know one another. Usually, in older quarters people know one another and strangers are easily identifies, especially since these quarters have many informers.
14. Ensuring that there has been no surveillance prior to the members entering the apartment.
15. Agreement among those living in the apartment on special ways of knocking on the door and special signs prior to entry into the building's main gate to indicate to those who wish to enter that the place is safe and not being monitored. Such signs include hanging out a towel, opening a curtain, placing a cushion in a special way, etc.
16. If there is a telephone in the apartment, calls should be answered in an agreed-upon manner by those who use the apartment. That would prevent mistakes that would, otherwise, lead to revealing the names and nature of the occupants.
17. For apartments, replace the locks and keys with new ones. As for the other entities (camps, shops, mosques) appropriate security precautions should be taken depending on the entity's importance and role in the work.

18. Apartments used for undercover work should not be visible from higher apartments in order not to expose the nature of the work.
19. In a new apartment, avoid talking loud because prefabricated ceilings and walls do not have the same thickness as those in old ones.
20. It is necessary to have at hand documents supporting the undercover [member]. In the case of a physician, there should be an actual medical diploma, membership in the union, the government permit, and the rest of the routine procedures known in that country.
21. The cover should blend well. For example, selecting a doctor's clinic in an area where there are clinics, or in a location suitable for it.
22. The cover of those who frequent the location should match the cover of that location. For example, a common laborer should not enter a fancy hotel because that would be suspicious and draw attention.

FIFTH LESSON: MEANS OF COMMUNICATION AND TRANSPORTATION

In the name of Allah, the merciful and compassionate:

It is well-known that in undercover operations, communication is the mainstay of the movement for rapid accomplishment. However, it is a double-edged sword: It can be to our advantage if we use it well and it can be a knife dug into our back if we do not consider and take the necessary security measures.

COMMUNICATION MEANS

The Military Organization in any Islamic group can, with its modest capabilities, use the following means: 1. The telephone 2. Meeting in-person 3. Messenger 4. Letters 5. Some modern devices, such as the facsimile and wireless. Communication may within the country, state, or even the county, in which case it is called local communication. When it extends between countries, it is called international communication.

SECRET COMMUNICATION IS LIMITED TO THE FOLLOWING TYPES

1. COMMON: It is a communication between two members of the Organization without being monitored by the opposing security apparatus. The common communication should be done under a certain cover and after inspecting the surveillance situation.
2. STANDBY: This replaces common communication when one of the two parties is unable to communicate with the other for some reason.
3. ALARM: Used when the opposing security apparatus discovers an undercover activity or undercover members. Based on this communication, the activity is stopped for a while,

all matters related to the activity are abandoned and the members are hidden from security personnel.

METHODS OF COMMUNICATION AMONG MEMBERS OF THE ORGANIZATION

1. Communication about undercover activity should be done using a good cover; it should also be quick, explicit, and pertinent. That is, just for talking only.
2. Prior to contacting his members, the commander of the cell should agree with each of them separately (the cell members should never meet all in one place and should not know one another) on a manner and means of communication with each other. Likewise, the chief of the Organization should use a similar technique with the branch commanders.

   Cell or cluster methods should be adopted by the Organization. It should be composed of many cells whose members do not know one another, so that if a cell member is caught the other cells would not be affected, and work would proceed normally.
3. A higher-ranking commander determines the type and method of communication with lower-ranking leaders.

FIRST MEANS: THE TELEPHONE

Because of significant technological advances, security measures for monitoring the telephone and broadcasting equipment have increased. Monitoring may be done by installing a secondary line or wireless broadcasting device on a telephone that relays the calls to a remote location. That is why the Organization takes security measures among its members who use this means of communication.

1. Communication should be carried out from public places. One should select telephones that are less suspicious to the security apparatus and are more difficult to monitor. It is preferable to use telephones in booths and on main streets.
2. Conversation should be coded or in general terms so as not to alert the person monitoring.
3. Periodically examine the telephone wire and receiver.
4. Telephone numbers should be memorized and not recorded. If the brother has to write them, he should do so using a code so they do not appear as telephone numbers (figures from a shopping list, etc.)
5. The telephone caller and person called should mention some words or sentences prior to bringing up the intended subject.
   The brother who is calling may misdial one of the digits and actually call someone else. The person called may claim that the call is for him, and the calling brother may start telling him work-related issues and reveal many things because of a minor error.
6. In a telephone conversation about undercover work, the voices should be changed and distorted.

7. When feasible, it is preferable to change telephone lines to allow direct access to local and international calls. That and proper cover facilitate communications and provide security protection not available when the central telephone station in the presence of many employees is used.
8. When a telephone is identified, the command and all parties who were using it should be notified as soon as possible in order to take appropriate measures.
9. When the command is certain that a particular telephone line is being monitored, it can exploit it by providing information that misleads the enemy and benefits the work plan.
10. If the Organization manages to obtain jamming devices, it should use them immediately.

SECOND MEANS: MEETING IN-PERSON

This is direct communication between the commander and a member of the Organization. During the meeting the following are accomplished.

1. Information exchange.
2. Giving orders and instructions.
3. Financing.
4. Member follow-up.

STAGES OF THE IN-PERSON MEETING

A. BEFORE THE MEETING

1. Designating the meeting location.

A. For stationary meetings:

- i. The location should be far from police stations and security centers.
- ii. Ease of transportation to the location.
- iii. Selecting the location prior to the meeting and learning all its details.
- iv. If the meeting location is an apartment, it should not be the first one, but one somewhere in the middle.
- v. The availability of many roads leading to the meeting location. That would provide easy escape in case the location was raided by security personnel.
- vi. The location should not be under suspicion.
- vii. The apartment where the meeting takes place should be on the ground floor, to facilitate escape.
- viii. The ability to detect any surveillance from that location.
- ix. When public transportation is used, one should alight at some distance from the meeting location and continue on foot. In the case of a private vehicle, one should park it far away or in a secure place so as to be able to maneuver it quickly at any time.

B. If the meeting location is not stationary, the following matters should be observed:
   i. The meeting location should be at the intersection of a large number of main and side streets to facilitate entry, exit, and escape.
   ii. The meeting location (ie a coffee shop) should not have members that might be dealing with the security apparatus.
   iii. The meeting should not be held in a crowded place because that would allow the security personnel to hide and monitor those who meet.
   iv. It is imperative to agree on an alternative location for the meeting in case meeting in the first is unfeasible. That holds whether the meeting place is stationary or not.

C. Those who meet in-person should do the following:
   i. Verifying the security situation of the location before the meeting.
   ii. Ensuring that there are no security personnel behind them or at the meeting place.
   iii. Not heading to the location directly.
   iv. Clothing and appearance should be appropriate for the meeting location.
   v. Verifying that private documents carried by the brother have appropriate cover.
   vi. Prior to the meeting, designing a security plan that specifies what the security personnel would be told in case the location were raided by them, and what the brothers

would resort to in dealing with the security personnel (fleeing, driving back…)

2. Finding a proper cover for the meeting. The cover:
   i. should blend well with the nature of the location.
   ii. should be believable to security personnel if they conduct a raid.
   iii. should not arouse the curiosity of those present.
   iv. should match the person's appearance and his financial/educational background.
   v. should have documents that support it.
   vi. Should provide reasons for the meeting (eg: one of the parties should have proof that he is an architect. The other should have documents as proof that he is a land owner. The architect has produced a construction plan for the land).
3. Specifying the meeting date and time.
   i. Specifying the hour of the meeting as well as the date.
   ii. Specifying the time of both parties' arrival and the time of the first party's departure.
   iii. Specifying how long the meeting will last.
   iv. Specifying an alternative date and time.
   v. Not allowing a long period of time between making the meeting arrangements and the meeting itself.
4. Defining special signals between those who meet.

If the two individuals meeting know one another's shape and appearance, it is sufficient to use a single safety sign.

The sitting and arriving individuals inform each other that there is no enemy surveillance. The sign may be keys, beads, a newspaper, or a scarf.

The two parties would agree on moving it in a special way so as not to attract the attention of those present.

IF THE INDIVIDUALS DO NOT KNOW ONE ANOTHER, THEY SHOULD DO THE FOLLOWING:

a. The initial sign for becoming acquainted may be that both of them wear a certain type of clothing or carry a certain item. These signs should be appropriate for the place, easily identified, and meet the purpose. The initial sign for becoming acquainted does not identify one person by another. It does that at a rate of 30%.
b. Safety Signal: It is given by the individual sitting in the meeting location to inform the second individual that the place is safe. The second person would reply through signals to inform the first that he is not being monitored. The signals are agreed upon previously and should not cause suspicion.
c. A second signal for getting acquainted is one in which the arriving person uses while sitting down. That signal may be a certain clause, a word, a sentence, or a gesture agreed upon previously, and should not cause suspicion for those who hear it or see it.

B. THE MEETING STAGE: The following measures should be taken:
   1. Caution during the meeting.
   2. Not acting unnaturally during the meeting in order not to raise suspicion.
   3. Not talking with either loud or very low voices (moderate).
   4. Not writing anything that has to do with the meeting.
   5. Agreeing on a security plan in case the enemy raids the location.

C. AFTER THE MEETING: The following measures should be taken:
   1. Not departing together, but each one separately.
   2. Not heading directly to the main road but through secondary ones.
   3. Not leaving anything in the meeting place that might indicate the identity or nature of those who met.

Meeting in-person has disadvantages, such as:
1. Allowing the enemy to capture those who are meeting.
2. Allowing them to take pictures of those who are meeting, record their conversation, and gather evidence against them.
3. Revealing the appearance of the commander to the other person. However, that may be avoided by taking the previously mentioned

measures such as disguising himself well and changing his appearance (glasses, wigs, etc.)

THIRD MEANS: THE MESSENGER

This is an intermediary between the sender and the receiver. The messenger should possess all characteristics mentioned in the first chapter regarding the Military Organization's member. These are the security measures that a messenger should take:

1. Knowledge of the person to whom he will deliver the message.
2. Agreement on special signals, exact date, and specific time.
3. Selecting a public street or place that does not raise suspicion.
4. Going through a secondary road that does not have check points.
5. Using public transportation (train, bus, etc) and disembarking before the main station. Likewise, embarking should not be done at the main station either, where there are a lot of security personnel and informants.
6. Complete knowledge of the location to which he is going.

FOURTH MEANS: LETTERS

Letters may be used as a method of communication between members and the Organization provided that the following security measures are taken:

1. It is forbidden to write any secret information in the letter. If one must do so, the writing should be done in general terms.
2. The letter should not be mailed from a post office to the sender's residence, but from a distant one.
3. The letter should not be sent directly to the receiver's address but to an inconspicuous location where there are many workers from your country. Afterward, the letter will be forwarded to the intended receiver (this is regarding the overseas-bound letter).
4. The sender's name and address on the envelope should be fictitious. In case the letters and their contents are discovered, the security apparatus would not be able to determine his name and address.
5. The envelope should not be transparent so as to reveal the letter inside.
6. The enclosed pages should not be many, so as not to raise suspicion.
7. The receiver's address should be written clearly so that the letter would not be returned.
8. Paying the post office box fees should not be forgotten.

FIFTH MEANS: FACSIMILE AND WIRELESS

Considering its modest capabilities and the pursuit by the security apparatus of its members and forces, the Islamic Military Organization cannot obtain these devices. In case the Organization is able to obtain them, firm security measures should be taken to secure communication between the members in the country and the command outside. These measures are:

1. The duration of the transmission should not exceed five minutes in order to prevent the enemy from pinpointing the device location.
2. The device should be placed in a location with high wireless frequency, such as close to a TV station, embassies, and consulates in order to prevent the enemy from identifying its location.
3. The brother, using the wireless device to contact his command outside the country, should disguise his voice.
4. The time of communication should be carefully specified.
5. The frequency should be changed from time to time.
6. The device should be frequently moved from one location to another.
7. Do not reveal your location to the entity for which you report.
8. The conversation should be in general terms so as not to raise suspicion.

TRANSPORTATION MEANS

The members of the Organization may move from one location to another using one of the following means:
a. Public transportation & b. Private transportation
Security Measures that Should be Observed in Public Transportation:

1. One should select public transportation that is not subject to frequent checking along the way, such as crowded trains or public buses.
2. Boarding should be done at a secondary station, as main stations undergo more careful surveillance. Likewise, embarkment should not be done at main stations.
3. The cover should match the general appearance (tourist bus, first-class train, second-class train, etc.)
4. The existence of documents supporting the cover.
5. Placing important luggage among the passengers' luggage without identifying the one who placed it. If it is discovered, its owner would not be arrested. In trains, it should be placed in a different car than that of the owner.
6. The brother traveling on a 'special mission' should not get involved in religious issues (advocating good or denouncing evil) or day-to-day matters (seat reservation…)
7. The brother traveling on a mission should not arrive in the destination country at night because then

travelers are few, and there are security parties and check points along the way.

8. When cabs are used, conversation of any kind should not be started with the driver because many cab drivers work for the security apparatus.
9. The brother should exercise extreme caution and apply all security measures to the members.

SECURITY MEASURES RELATED TO PRIVATE TRANSPORTATION

Private transportation includes: cars, motorcycles

B. Cars motorcycles used in overt activity:

1. One should possess the proper permit and not violate traffic rules in order to avoid trouble with the police.
2. The location of the vehicle should be secure so that the security apparatus would not confiscate it.
3. The vehicle make and model should be appropriate for the brother's cover.
4. The vehicle should not be used in special military operations unless the Organization has no other choice.

B. Cars and motorcycles used in covert activity:

1. Attention should be given to permits and the traffic rules in order to avoid trouble and reveal their actual mission.
2. The vehicle should not be left in suspicious places (deserts, mountains). If it must be, then the work

should be performed at suitable times when no one would keep close watch or follow it.

3. The vehicle should be purchased using forged documents so that getting to its owners would be prevented once it is discovered.
4. For the sake of continuity, have only one brother in charge of selling.
5. While parking somewhere, one should be in a position to move quickly and flee in case of danger.
6. The car or motorcycle color should be changed before the operation and returned to the original after the operation.
7. The license plate number and country name should be falsified. Furthermore, the digits should be numerous in order to prevent anyone from spotting and memorizing them.
8. The operation vehicle should not be taken to large gasoline stations so that it would not be detected by the security apparatus.

SIXTH LESSON: TRAINING

The following security measures should be taken during training:

The place should have the following specifications:

1. Distance from the populated areas with the availability of living necessities.
2. Availability of medical services during the training.
3. The place should be suitable for the type of training (physical fitness, shooting, tactics).

4. No one except the trainers and trainees should know about the place.
5. The place should have many roads and entrances.
6. The place should be visited at suitable times.
7. Hiding any traces of the training immediately afterward.
8. Guarding the place during the training.
9. Appropriateness of the existing facilities for the number of training members.
10. Exclusion of anyone who is not connected with the training.
11. Taking all security measures regarding the establishment.
12. Distance of the place from police stations, public establishments, and the eyes of informants.
13. The place should not be situated in such a way that the training and trainees can be seen from another location.

<u>The Trainees</u>

1. Before proceeding to the training place, all security measures connected with an undercover individual should be taken. Meanwhile, during training at the place, personnel safety should be ensured.
2. Selecting the trainees carefully.
3. The trainees should not know one another.
4. The small size of groups that should be together during the training (7-10 individuals).
5. The trainees should not know the training place.
6. Establishing a training plan for each trainee.

The Trainers

All measures taken with regard to the commanders apply also to the trainers. Also, the following should be applied:

1. Fewness of the trainers in the training place. Only those conducting the training should be there, in order not to subject the training team to the risk of security exposure.
2. Not revealing the identity of the trainer to the trainees.
3. Keeping a small ratio of trainees to trainer.
4. The training team members should not know one another.

WEAPONS: MEASURES RELATED TO BUYING AND TRANSPORTING THEM

Prior to dealing with weapons, whether buying, transporting, or storing them, it is essential to establish a careful, systematic and firm security plan that deals with all stages. It is necessary to divide that task into stages: First Stage: Prior to Purchase; Second Stage: Purchasing; Third Stage: Transport; Fourth Stage: Storage.

Prior to Purchase Stage:

a. In-depth knowledge of the place where weapons will be purchased, together with its entrances and exits.

b. Verifying there are no informants or security personnel at the place where purchasing will take place.
c. The place should be far from police stations and government establishments.
d. Not proceeding to the purchasing place directly by the main road, but on secondary streets.
e. Performing the exercises to detect surveillance.
f. One's appearance and clothing should be appropriate for the place where purchasing will take place.
g. The purchasing place should not be situated in such a way that the seller and buyer can be seen from another location. To the contrary, the purchasing place should be such that the seller and buyer can see the surrounding area.
h. Determining a suitable cover for being in that place.
i. The place should not be crowded because that would facilitate the police hiding among people, monitoring the arms receiving, and consequently arresting the brother purchasing.
j. In case one of the parties is unable to arrive, it is essential to prearrange an alternative place and time with the seller.
k. Selecting a time suitable for the purchase that does not raise suspicion.
l. Prior to purchasing, the seller should be tested to ensure that he is not an agent of the security apparatus.
m. Preparing a place for storage prior to purchasing.

<u>The Purchase Stage:</u>

a. Verifying that the weapons are in working condition.
b. Not paying the seller the price for the weapons before viewing, inspecting, and testing them.
c. Not telling the seller the mission for which the weapons are being purchased.
d. Extreme caution should be used during the purchasing operation in the event of any unnatural behavior by the seller or those around you.
e. Not lengthening the time spent with the seller. It is important to depart immediately after purchasing the weapon.

<u>Transport Stage</u>:

a. Avoid main roads where check points are common.
b. Choose a suitable time for transporting the weapons.
c. Observers should proceed on the road ahead of the transportation vehicle for early warning in case of an emergency.
d. Not proceeding directly to the storage place until after verifying there is no surveillance.
e. During the transport stage, weapons should be hidden in a way that is inconspicuous and difficult to find.
f. The route for transporting the weapons should be determined very carefully.
g. Verifying the legality of the vehicle, performing its maintenance, checking its gasoline and water levels etc.

h. Driving the car normally in order to prevent accidents.

Storage Stage:

a. In order to avoid repeated transporting, suitable storage places should be selected. In case the materials are bombs or detonators, they should be protected from extreme heat and humidity.
b. Explosive materials and detonators should be separated and stored apart from each other.
c. Caution should be exercised when putting detonators in the arsenal.
d. Lubricating the weapons and placing them in wooden or plastic crates. The ammunition should be treated likewise.

When selecting an arsenal, consider the following:

1. The arsenal should not be in well-protected areas, or close to parks or public places.
2. The arsenal should not be in a "no-man's land."
3. The arsenal should not be in an apartment previously used for suspicious activities and often frequented by security personnel.
4. The arsenal should not be a room that is constantly used and cannot be given up by family members who do not know the nature of the father or husband's work.
5. The apartment selected as an arsenal should be owned by the Organization or rented on a long-term basis.

6. The brother responsible for storage should not visit the arsenal frequently, nor toy with the weapons.
7. The arsenal keeper should record in a book all weapons, explosive materials, and ammunition. That book should be coded and well secured.
8. Only the arsenal keeper and the commander should know the location of the arsenal.
9. It is necessary to prepare alternative arsenals and not leave any leads in the original arsenal to the alternative ones.

As you can conclude, terrorists are well trained and well informed on how to plan and execute an operation. In the next chapter we will take a look at how the policing in America has evolved over the past century, and what law enforcement must do in the future to defeat the enemy lurking on the borders of our cities and towns.

CHAPTER 4
GOOD COPS AND BAD COPS

Before one can fully understand the importance of the changes police departments will be required to make in order to meet the challenges of the next century, we need to look back in history and review how policing methodologies evolved in the last century.

Throughout history our nation's leaders have resisted creating a national police force similar to police forces in England and other nations, for fear of encouraging the creation of a "quasi-army" under one-command authority.

Police agencies across America historically have operated independent from each other and from federal control. All of America's police departments differ in size, uniforms, the way they establish a chain of command and in crime fighting methodologies.

From the 1800's to the mid 1960's, the police in America were well respected. Cops were tough, but only on the bad guys. It was not uncommon for people to see police officers out of their patrol cars, walking in neighborhoods, and chatting with shopkeepers and kids.

In the 20th Century, policing methodologies evolved from cops patrolling on the beat, to cops patrolling in police cars, to cops patrolling in the sky and on the sea, and then returning to the "beat cop" via community policing methodologies.

When the United States went to war with North Vietnam in 1964, the way the American people viewed their police changed dramatically. The war divided the rich and poor, the black man and white man, and ultimately the police and the people.

Nearly half the population from one end of America to the other went to "war" with the police in confrontations that erupted as a result of Vietnam. Indeed, American law enforcement had a public relations nightmare on their hands.

Soon after the Vietnam War began, thousands of young American men were drafted into military service. Police departments suffered manpower shortages, forcing them to curtail, and in most cases, totally eliminate the "cop on the beat." Almost overnight, policing methodologies changed from proactive to reactive. The positive contact beat cops were having with the public was soon to become a thing of the past.

As the war continued and thousands of American neighborhood boys were being killed in the jungles of Vietnam, the American people began to protest against the government. There was flag burning, riots, and marches all over the nation.

The first protests began on college campuses by anti-war students. Soon teachers and professors marched with the students. Finally, moms, dads, and citizens from all walks of life organized marches against the war in every city and town across America.

When a war is protracted, the first thing that usually suffers is public support. Without the public behind its military, victory will give way to defeat. The Vietnam

War lasted ten years, cost 50,000 American lives, became America's first military defeat in history, and greatly divided the nation.

Had U.S. government leaders followed the advice written on the pages of Sun Tzu's Art of War, much pain and suffering inflicted on the people of the United States would have been spared; *"It is never beneficial for a nation to have a military operation continue for a long time."*

During the 1960's, the "friendly cop" on the beat with the neatly pressed uniform gleaming in the sunlight, chatting with parents, kids, and shopkeepers, was transformed into the cop wearing a helmet, carrying tear gas, and using physical and deadly force against the very people he is called to "protect and serve."

Many people who witnessed this transformation in policing would not argue that in numerous instances the police had to use aggressive tactics against violent protestors. But the overwhelming majority of Americans saw things differently.

Police officials who believed that get tough policies on protesters would result in a decrease in violence were given a wake-up call when many protestors began to target them, calling police "pigs," believing that the police represented U.S. government policy toward Vietnam.

Large numbers of American people were now at "war" not only in the green jungles of Southeast Asia, but also in the asphalt jungles of our nation's streets against another "enemy," the police.

In 1968, the Vietnam War was at its peak. During this period of time while tens of thousands of Americans were protesting against the war, presidential national conventions were being held. The people opposed to the war believed they had an opportunity to make a dramatic change in government policy toward Vietnam by electing a new president and a new congress to office. Hence, they took their protests from the streets of America to the political party conventions where the presidential candidates could hear first-hand their collective voices in opposition to the war.

The Democratic Party held its national convention in Chicago, Illinois in July 1968. As thousands of delegates attended the convention to nominate a candidate for president, tens of thousands of anti-war protestors swarmed the streets just outside the convention hall in downtown Chicago.

Although there were numerous agitators and instigators looking for trouble, most of the demonstrators were college students, parents of men serving in Vietnam, and politicians. For the first time since the American Revolution, a cross section of America's society, representing every religion, ethnicity and economic level, converged on one city, for one cause, at one time.

On the evening of the convention, television news crews began broadcasting numerous speeches from inside the hall. However, rumors were spreading that the crowds outside convention hall were getting restless. As Americans and people from all over the world watched the news coverage from inside convention hall, some news crews decided to go outside into the streets to see what was going on.

Reporters attempting to leave from inside convention hall were met by Chicago police officers and told they were not allowed outside, and to return to their seats. Arguments erupted and some news reporters ran past the police and out onto the streets.

What these reporters saw happening on those streets, shocked them. The violence they witnessed and broadcasted shocked the entire world. Within minutes of the initial broadcasts of the violence on the streets of Chicago, dozens of news crews were rushing out of convention hall, and instead of the convention's "pomp" and "sparkling glitter" being broadcasted worldwide, people were now viewing the American police in action, complements of Mayor Richard Daly, and the Chicago Police Department.

Tens of thousands of people were chanting; *"The whole world is watching.*" Scenes of police wielding nightsticks on heads, backs, and legs of men and women, young and old alike, filled television screens. Police were punching kids and dragging them from their cars as viewers watched in horror.

For the first time in American history, with the exception of unwarranted police violence against America's black people, American citizens had come under attack from their own protectors.

Chicago police officials attempted to justify the actions of their officers during hearings and investigations held by numerous government agencies soon after the violence ceased. But citizens throughout the nation who witnessed the carnage and beatings perpetrated by unlawful police actions, did not accept the shallow explanations of Chicago police officials. The Chicago Police Department sent a chilling and long lasting message to Americans; that the police in the United States were no longer a friend of the people.

The public backlash against the Chicago Police Department revealed that police in America had lost touch with the public as a result of replacing proactive policing methodologies, with a methodology of policing that isolated the police from the people. The American people would soon learn that police nationwide had embraced an "us against them," mindset.

It took nearly thirty years for America's law enforcement community to publicly admit that the Chicago Police Department's actions against the people of their city in the summer of 1968 were criminal at the very least.

Fortunately, in the 1970's, progressive political leaders and police chiefs throughout the nation knew that something had to be done to change the way the people viewed the police. Many fine police leaders worked hard to re-establish ties with their communities. But in 1973, one tragic incident involving anti-war protestors and the police brought their efforts to a crashing end.

In the mid-seventies police and students on college campuses were routinely clashing over the Vietnam War. In 1973, protests got so bad on one college campus that National Guard troops were called to assist the police. Within an hour after the army set foot on the grounds of Kent State University, several student protestors lie dead on the campus grounds. They were shot down by some of the National Guard troops. An appalled American public blamed the police for this tragic confrontation. It was by far the worst clash between unarmed students and law enforcement ever recorded in American history. As a result of this incident, thousands of Americans had declared "open warfare" on the police.

For the next few years, riots, civil unrest, flag burning and police shootings rapidly increased; and news broadcasts carried stories about cops being assaulted, beaten, and shot by mobs. It was an ugly time of unrest for America.

When the Vietnam War was coming to a close, a new breed of cop was emerging in the police ranks. With peace at hand and better-educated men and women joining the police ranks, the time was ripe to make changes in the way the police in the United States did business. Unfortunately, it would be another twenty years before good cops would replace a lot of bad cops.

CHAPTER 5
EVOLUTION IN POLICING

In the mid 1970s, the buzzword in police vocabulary was "Safe Neighborhoods." The federal government poured millions of dollars into police agencies that hired cops and assigned them specifically to "walking the beat" in crime troubled neighborhoods.

Police leadership believed that returning cops to "beat patrol" would break down the wall of separation between the people and the police. Law enforcement officials were also convinced that by putting cops on walking patrols, police intelligence capabilities would increase with a net result of a reduced crime rate.

To some degree, the "Safe Neighborhoods" program reduced crime in a number of cities. However, the program did not have significant impact on breaking down the wall of separation between the people and the police. What was suppose to be a policing methodology to bring the police and people together, became an added burden for police departments to fund, and a larger problem for the people to cope with, as poorly trained and insensitive cops infiltrated their neighborhoods.

Federal and local governments tried to use "Safe Neighborhood Units" as a quick fix to improve police-community relations. Unfortunately, most officers assigned to "Safe Neighborhoods" programs were not trained in communication skills, cultural diversity, or the use of common sense. Most cops assigned to walking beats viewed the program as a means to punish them.

"Safe Neighborhoods" was not a complete failure. The program did break the reactive policing mentality of many police administrators, forcing them to return to proactive policing methodologies. The "Safe Neighborhoods" program was a seed that required a lot of "water" before the fruits of its vine would flourish two decades later.

During the 1980's policing evolved into hostage negotiators, SWAT Teams, computers, and robo-cop equipment. Police leadership nationwide was convinced that investing in high-tech equipment and training their cops into specialized fields would result in low crime rates and much needed public support for the cop on the street.

Many law enforcement leaders were proven right about some of the investments they made in high-tech crime fighting equipment. Arrest statistics were up all over the nation and police departments were able to identify criminals, track them down, and bring them to justice, in record time.

However, along with this success came a major failure. Most of the high-tech gadgetry purchased and used effectively by law enforcement officials were reactive tools. Not much of it prevented crime.

A national study on crime in America revealed that crime had actually increased during this time period. The public image of the police remained negative. And police officials found themselves working overtime to improve police-community relations.

In the early 1990's, with most police departments working toward building positive police-community relations, the law enforcement community nationwide was rocked by a widely published incident viewed by millions of people around the world.

Los Angeles police officers made a routine motor vehicle stop of a car driven by a black man named Rodney King. Somehow, this routine stop got out of control after several police officers responded to the area where Mr. King was pulled over. Within minutes, police had King on the ground. The officers were not aware that a citizen not far from the scene was videotaping them. The videotape was sent to the press, and the world soon witnessed nearly a dozen LAPD officers beating Rodney King to the ground, hitting him over 59 times with nightsticks, and using a taser gun to subdue him. In the eyes of the average "John Q. Public," Rodney King was viciously beaten by out of control cops. In the eyes of minorities, the cops had declared war on black America.

There is much controversy as to whether the force used on Rodney King by the police was justified. According to the police, King was violent with them before the video camera started rolling. But regardless of anyone's opinion, the public verdict on the LAPD was in! And public opinion of the police in America had reached an all time low. The streets of the nation were ripe for another "war" between the people and their protectors.

After the LAPD officers who beat King went to trial and where acquitted, minorities took to the streets and burned houses and stores. They looted, robbed and beat dozens of non-minority people. Citizens all over the world viewed television news scenes of innocent people being dragged from their cars and beaten to near death by mobs.

LAPD Chief Darryl Gates ordered his officers away from the chaos and directed them to form a perimeter just outside the "circle of destruction." The chief's idea was to contain the people to their own neighborhoods. If rioters attempted to cross the perimeter established by the police, a well-armed force would confront them. Containing the destruction worked, but it also allowed rioters to beat, maim, and kill innocent people at will.

The LAPD failed to "protect and serve" the people of Los Angeles during one of America's most critical hours. The entire world witnessed this failure. Many people across America viewed the police as enemies of the public and soon thousands of people throughout America would be carrying a new weapon they intended to use against the police-a video camera.

As time went on, videos of police beating people surfaced everywhere. Violent cops caught on tape were prosecuted and sent to prison by victimized white people, black people, and other minorities. The wall of separation between the police and the people reached an all time high. In many cities police were heckled and assaulted. The "Safe Neighborhoods" programs of the 70's became "the crime ridden streets" of the 90's.

Every good cop knew that something had to be done to turn the tide of negative publicity and public resentment against the police to a more positive relationship. Many cops across the nation knew that only they could successfully break down the wall separating them from the people. Good cops had to step up and speak out about the failures of America's law enforcement profession, and the polarization its leadership created between the police and the people.

Police professionals had to let the people of America know how they intended to change public and police attitudes, mend fences, and build new bridges between the police and the people.

It was not until the late 90's that police officers began to reach out to the people through the implementation of 1950's community policing methodologies.

Police-community partnerships were created, civilian police academies were organized, junior police academies for kids were formed, ride-a-long programs were scheduled, and dozens of police-community relations programs were advanced in cities all across America. After thirty years of bad relations between the people and the police, law enforcement was succeeding in winning back the hearts, minds, and support of the American people. The greatest asset the police enjoyed as a result of this restored relationship with the public was the mass amount of information and intelligence average citizens were feeding them, via programs like Neighborhood Watch and Citizens Patrol.

Arrests in the 90's were skyrocketing as a result of the "extended eyes and ears" of citizens participating in crime watch programs. As arrest rates leveled off, crime rates were reflecting a downward trend. The people were now cheering the police, instead of heckling them.

Police nationwide stayed the course and maintained strong community partnerships with the public. The U.S. government poured millions of dollars of grant money into police departments that created police-public partnerships. These investments paid off in safer cities and strong police-community relations. However, in early 2000, the police were once again facing difficult times. Minorities were claiming that police nationwide were engaging in racial profiling. Several incidents involving the police and minorities took a nationwide stage.

Day after day, and week after week, the American people once again were reading about "how bad" the police were. But to the credit of many citizens and police officers who worked night and day to maintain the programs created in the late 90's which bought the police and the people together, a repeat of the days when the people and the police were at "war," was prevented.

However, racial profiling became the number one story carried by television, radio, and newsprint all across the nation. As a result of this wave of bad publicity, American law enforcement was bracing for what some criminal justice leaders predicted would be the most turbulent time in history for police officers throughout the nation. America was preparing for another Chicago and Los Angeles. But unforeseen events would prevent a repeat of the violence of the 60's, 70's, and 80's because another type of violence that would shock the world, would strike within America's borders, and present a view of today's police as America's greatest heroes of all time.

On Tuesday morning, September 11th 2001, America went to war. Within a two-hour period terrorists had successfully carried out a major attack on the United States, killing nearly 3,000 people in New York, Northern Virginia, and Pennsylvania. Soon, the programs built by the police and the people for nearly two decades would disappear. But their strong relationship would not disappear. In fact, it would strengthen like never before in history. On this new "day of infamy," the police were hailed as America's heroes. The images and complaints about police brutality, racial profiling, and unfair treatment of the public virtually disappeared overnight. The people knew that the only force standing between them and terror were their local cops. Americans knew that no one except their neighborhood cops would have the courage to fight terrorism on their streets. The people knew that they had to support their cops at all costs. Things were now different. We were at war!

America declared a global war on terrorism. The police, as well as the military, needed every weapon at their disposal to meet the challenges that lie ahead. The president began to give law enforcement the weapons they needed when he started signing legislation designed to strengthen both military might and police authority.

Within days after this attack, new laws were proposed and directives were issued by the president of the United States to strengthen America's law enforcement efforts by bringing together all of America's resources in the fight against terrorism.

Hence, another evolution in policing had arrived. The community cop who was "walking the beat" and working in partnership with neighborhood people to address quality of life issues would again disappear.

Over the horizon of America's law enforcement landscape was the type of policing no one, not the police, nor the public, wanted to see take root in this nation. But war brings unexpected change. In the case of law enforcement and the war on terrorism, the way police would do business in the days ahead would dramatically change.

In June of 2002, President George W. Bush recommended that the Office of Homeland Security become a cabinet level department which would coordinate numerous functions related to terrorism in America. He also recommended that Congress change old laws that limited federal and local law enforcement agencies from sharing information with the military and Department of Defense intelligence agencies. He recommended sweeping legislation that would restructure numerous federal agencies, including the FBI, CIA, INS, and U.S. Coast Guard.

The following Presidential Executive Order set the stage for how America and its police forces would fight the war on terrorism in the future. The fruit of the president's labor was born in January of 2003 when the Department of Homeland Security was officially created. (Elements applicable to local police are cited and underlined. Elements not applicable to local police are deleted from the text).

Executive Order 13228
Establishing the Office of Homeland Security
And the
Homeland Security Council

I: By the authority vested in me as President by the Constitution and the laws of the United States of America, it is hereby ordered as follows:

<u>Section 1. Establishment</u>. I hereby establish within the Executive Office of the President, an Office of Homeland Security to be headed by the Assistant to the President for Homeland Security.

Sec. <u>2. Mission.</u> The mission of the Office shall be to develop and coordinate the implementation of a comprehensive national strategy to secure the United States from terrorist threats or attacks. The Office shall perform the functions necessary to carry out this mission, including the functions specified in section 3 of this order.

Sec. <u>3. Functions.</u> The functions of the Office shall be to coordinate the executive branch's efforts to detect, prepare for, prevent, protect against, respond to, and recover from terrorist attacks within the United States.

(a) National Strategy. The Office shall work with executive departments and agencies, State and local governments, and private entities to ensure the adequacy of the national strategy for detecting, preparing for, preventing, protecting against, responding to, and recovering from terrorist threats or attacks within the United States and shall periodically review and coordinate revisions to that strategy as necessary.

(b) Detection. The Office shall identify priorities and coordinate efforts for collection and analysis of information within the United States regarding threats of terrorism against the United States and activities of terrorists or terrorist groups within the United States. The Office also shall identify, in coordination with the Assistant to the President for National Security Affairs, priorities for collection of intelligence outside the United States regarding threats of terrorism within the United States.

I: In performing these functions, the Office shall work with Federal, State, and local agencies, as appropriate, to: (a) facilitate collection from State and local governments and private entities of information pertaining to terrorist threats or activities within the United States; (b) deleted; (c) coordinate efforts to ensure that all executive departments and agencies that have intelligence collection responsibilities have sufficient technological capabilities and resources to collect intelligence. (d) coordinate development of monitoring protocols and equipment for use in detecting the release of biological, chemical, and radiological hazards; and (e) ensure that, to the extent permitted by law, all appropriate and necessary intelligence and law enforcement information relating to homeland security is disseminated to and exchanged among appropriate executive departments and agencies responsible for homeland security and, where appropriate for reasons of homeland security, promote exchange of such information with and among State and local governments and private entities.

II: Executive departments and agencies shall, to the extent permitted by law, make available to the Office all information relating to terrorist threats and activities within the United States.

(a) Preparedness. The Office of Homeland Security shall coordinate national efforts to prepare for and mitigate the consequences of terrorist threats or attacks within the United States. In performing this function, the Office shall work with Federal, State, and local agencies, and private entities, as appropriate, to: (i) review and assess the adequacy of the portions of all Federal emergency response plans that pertain to terrorist threats or attacks within the United States; (ii) coordinate domestic exercises and simulations designed to assess and practice systems that would be called upon to respond to a terrorist threat or attack within the United States and coordinate programs and activities for training Federal, State, and local employees who would be called upon to respond to such a threat or attack; (iii) deleted; (iv) coordinate Federal assistance to State and local authorities and nongovernmental organizations to prepare for and respond to terrorist threats or attacks within the United States; (v) ensure that national preparedness programs and activities for terrorist threats or attacks are developed and are regularly evaluated under appropriate standards and that resources are allocated to improving and sustaining preparedness based on such evaluations; and (vi) ensure the readiness and coordinated deployment of Federal response teams to respond to terrorist threats or attacks, working with the Assistant to the President for National Security Affairs, when appropriate.

(b) Prevention. The Office shall coordinate efforts to prevent terrorist attacks within the United States. In performing this function, the Office shall work with Federal, State, and local agencies, and private entities, as appropriate. (i) deleted; (ii) deleted (iii) deleted.

(c) Protection: The Office shall coordinate efforts to protect the United States and its critical infrastructure from the consequences of terrorist attacks. In performing this function, the Office shall work with Federal, State, and local agencies, and private entities, as appropriate, to: (i) strengthen measures for protecting energy production, transmission, and distribution services and critical facilities; other utilities; telecommunications; facilities that produce, use, store, or dispose of nuclear material; and other critical infrastructure services and critical facilities within the United States from terrorist attack; (ii) coordinate efforts to protect critical public and privately owned information systems within the United States from terrorist attack; (iii) develop criteria for reviewing whether appropriate security measures are in place at major public and privately owned facilities within the United States; (iv) coordinate domestic efforts to ensure that special events determined by appropriate senior officials to have national significance are protected from terrorist attack; (v) coordinate efforts to protect transportation systems within the United States, including railways, highways, shipping, ports and waterways, and airports and civilian aircraft, from terrorist attack; (vi) coordinate efforts to protect United States livestock, agriculture, and systems for the provision of water and food for human use and consumption from terrorist attack; and (vii) coordinate efforts to prevent unauthorized access to, development of, and unlawful importation into the United States of, chemical, biological, radiological, nuclear, explosive, or other related materials that have the potential to be used in terrorist attacks.

(d) Response and Recovery. The Office shall coordinate efforts to respond to and promote recovery from terrorist threats or attacks within the United States. In performing this function, the Office shall work with Federal, State, and local agencies, and private entities, as appropriate, to: (i) coordinate efforts to ensure restoration of transportation systems, energy production, transmission, and distribution systems; telecommunications; other utilities; and other critical infrastructure facilities after disruption by a terrorist threat or attack; (ii) coordinate efforts to ensure rapid restoration of public and private critical information systems after disruption by a terrorist threat or attack; (iii) deleted; (iv) coordinate Federal plans and programs to provide medical, financial, and other assistance to victims of terrorist attacks and their families; and (v) coordinate containment and removal of biological, chemical, radiological, explosive, or other hazardous materials in the event of a terrorist threat or attack involving such hazards and coordinate efforts to mitigate the effects of such an attack. (e) & (f) deleted; (g) Cooperation with State and Local Governments and Private Entities. The Office shall encourage and invite the participation of State and local governments and private entities, as appropriate, in carrying out the Office's functions. (h & i Deleted. Section 4, 5, 6,7,8,9, deleted).

In January 2003, Governor Tom Ridge became the first Secretary of Homeland Security. The president and Mr. Ridge began to address many issues related to laws governing military-civil police partnerships.

In January 2005, former U.S. Attorney General Michael Chertoff became the second Secretary of Homeland Security as President Bush began his second term.

CHAPTER 6
POSSE COMITATUS

President Bush and Governor Ridge knew that as time moved on police departments across the nation were going to have to build partnerships with the United States Military, the Department of Defense, and other national security organizations, in order to effectively combat terrorism in our homeland. These partnerships would focus on the collection of intelligence, obtaining military assistance in keeping order, tracking down suspected terrorists, and training police officers in anti-terrorism tactics.

Developing civil-military partnerships is a difficult matter because of the way current laws are written. Although military and civilian police partnerships can be created, they must adhere to strict governmental regulations.

The two most important laws police officials should become familiar with are, the Posse Comitatus Act and Intelligence Oversight Laws of the United States. Understanding these laws will help local police department officials forge valuable relationships with the FBI, the military, and other federal agencies.

THE POSSE COMITATUS ACT

The Posse Comitatus Act prohibits use of military personnel to execute the civil laws of the US, "except in cases and under circumstances expressly authorized by the Constitution or Act of Congress." Violation of the Act carries with it criminal liability and the possibility of a fine and imprisonment. The primary prohibition of the Posse Comitatus Act is against direct military involvement in law enforcement activities. Generally, court interpretations have held that military support short of actual search, seizure, arrest, or similar confrontation with civilians, (e.g. traditional law enforcement functions) is not a violation of the act.

In 1981, and in subsequent years, Congress codified a number of court interpretations in 10 USC 371-381, Military Support for Civilian Law Enforcement Agencies. In so doing, military commanders could feel confident that the support they provided to civilian law enforcement, particularly in the counter-drug area, would be legal. While these statutes are frequently called "exceptions" to the PCA, in fact, only one, 10 USC 374, expanded the court-set boundaries of the PCA. That statute permitted military forces to operate and maintain equipment.

Military departments may provide training to federal, state, and local civilian law enforcement officials and may include training in the operation and maintenance of equipment made available. Additionally, in the counter drug arena, additional legislative authority permits training of law enforcement personnel engaged in counter drug activities. Counter drug training support also requires the approval of higher authority. Nonetheless, judge advocates and their commanders usually proceed cautiously with requests for training support. For prudent reasons, and based on Special Operations Forces experiences in connection with the Bureau of Alcohol, Tobacco, and Firearms raid on the Branch Davidian Complex in Waco, TX in February of 1993, the Special Operations Command (USSOCOM) has limited the training it provides to basic military training, e.g. basic marksmanship, rappelling, fast rope, patrolling, mission planning, survival skills, land navigation, medical/combat lifesaver, and detection and avoidance of improvise/explosive devices, and advanced training such as sniper training and military Operations in Urban Terrain (MOUT). Advanced MOUT, Close Quarters Battle/Close Quarters Combat (CQB/CQC) are not permitted.

A legal review should be given to all law enforcement requests for support and they must be approved under the oversight of a general officer. More importantly, any requests to assist law enforcement agencies that will result in a planned event with the potential for confrontation with named individuals/groups or use of lethal force must be forwarded to the Secretary of Defense (SECDEF). 10 USC 375 emphasizes the outer limit of DOD support by requiring Secretary of Defense (SECDEF) to prescribe regulations prohibiting the direct participation of any service member (Army, Navy, Air Force, or Marine Corps) in a search, seizure, arrest, or similar activity, unless otherwise authorized by law.

DOD Directive 5525.5 is the implementing regulation and lists these "similar activities," e.g.

interrogation, surveillance, undercover work, informant work, and investigation.

The traditional exceptions to the PCA include the following: (1) Constitutional exception: Limited presidential authority in cases of emergency and to protect federal property. 2) Civil Disturbance Statutes: Permit use of federal troops to restore order. (3) Military Support for Civilian Law Enforcement Agencies Statutes & (4) Military Purpose Doctrine: Permits use of military personnel in a law enforcement role when primary purpose is a military one. Most often used in joint criminal investigations by military criminal investigative personnel and civilian law enforcement agencies.

The key phrase in the Posse Comitatus Act is "to execute the laws". Three different court interpretations have emerged from federal courts regarding what this language means.

In United States v. Jaramillo, 380 F. Supp 1375 (1974), the court looked to whether the conduct of the military "pervaded the activities" of civilian law enforcement.

In United States v. Red Feather, 392 F. Supp 916 (1975), the court held that executing the laws meant "direct active use" of military personnel.

In United States v. MacArthur, 419 F. Supp 186 (1976), the court decided that execution of the laws meant subjecting citizens to military authority which was "regulatory, proscriptive, or compulsory" in nature.

In United States v. Yunis, 681 F. Supp 891 (1988), the court applied the analysis from United States v.

MacArthur and reaffirmed the "regulatory, proscriptive, or compulsory" test.

All three tests may be applied to a single situation, and if the activity in question meets any of the tests, the court may determine that the Act itself has been violated. Note however, that no one has ever been convicted of a Posse Comitatus Act violation. Of greater likelihood, although also rare, is that the court may invoke the exclusionary rule in the case of a PCA violation, or that military personnel may be held civilly liable. A change in laws is forthcoming to make it easier for the military to assist law enforcement agencies and visa versa.

Major R. Barry Cronin, USMC, wrote an excellent analysis on the Posse Comitatus Act in which he explained, *"That if a cross-section of police chiefs were polled concerning their understanding of the Posse Comitatus Act, most would likely answer that the act prohibits U.S. military personnel from performing civilian law enforcement functions. However, to assume that Posse Comitatus prevents law enforcement agencies from obtaining any military support would be a mistake. In fact, several exceptions to the general prohibition exist, and civilian police organizations should not be reluctant to seek the military's help in certain circumstances.*

Major Cronin's article provides an overview of the type of military support available to civilian law enforcement agencies. He describes briefly the procedures for requesting military assistance, depending on the type and amount of support desired.

His analysis of this act and other writings can be reviewed in more depth, on the world-wide-web. The following is on the WWW for public consumption.

PERMISSIBLE DIRECT ASSISTANCE

By: Major Barry, Cronin, USMC

As a general rule, the Posse Comitatus Act restricts direct use of military personnel in civilian law enforcement operations. Direct assistance is defined as: 1) A search or seizure; 2) an arrest, apprehension, stop and frisk, or similar activity; or 3) the use of military personnel for surveillance or pursuit of individuals, or as undercover agents, informants, investigators, or interrogators.

Despite these restrictions, it is military policy to try to cooperate with civilian law enforcement officials to the maximum extent possible, depending upon national security and military preparedness, the tradition of limiting direct military involvement in civilian law enforcement activities, and the requirements of applicable law.

Even so, direct assistance is permissible when it is with the primary purpose of furthering a military or foreign affairs function of the United States, regardless of incidental benefits to civilian authorities. Direct assistance must support military interests.

Police chiefs, especially those with jurisdictions near major military installations, should be aware of this important exception and of the various forms of military assistance available locally.

TYPES OF AVAILABLE ASSISTANCE TO POLICE DEPARTMENTS

Military Working Dog Teams

The most widely requested form of military assistance is the military working dog (MWD) teams, which are located at almost every major Department of Defense (DOD) installation in the United States.

Normally, military bases have both explosive and drug detector dog teams available for use by civilian law enforcement with the understanding that military commitments will usually take precedence over civilian requests.

Every year, scores of civilian police agencies take advantage of firing ranges, combat towns, and other military training facilities. Depending on the size of the military installation, these facilities can vary from a standard, small arms requalification range to a full-scale combat town where police tactical units can practice in a realistic, urban setting.

There are also demolition ranges, as well as training areas where teams can conduct a variety of outside exercises. Additionally, office spaces and buildings may be used for traditional classroom training. And, if available, military instructors may also be used to train civilian law enforcement personnel.

Expert Advice/Technical Assistance

The military is authorized to provide expert advice to civilian law enforcement agencies. There is no restriction on this kind of support so long as military personnel do not participate directly in civilian law enforcement activities.

<u>Equipment and Personnel</u>

Military equipment can be loaned to civilian law enforcement agencies on a temporary basis to support on-going operations and training. Approval for these requests is handled on a case-by-case basis.

In addition, personnel may also be requested in situations where it would be impractical from a cost or time perspective to train civilian personnel to operate and/or to maintain equipment.

For example, a few years ago, a local police department requested assistance from a nearby Marine Corps base concerning a homicide case. Eleven Marines, using minesweepers, were assigned to help the local police department conduct an area search for the homicide weapon. In this case, it would have been highly impractical to train local police department members on how to use mine sweepers properly. In such cases, however, service members operating or maintaining equipment should not be placed in positions where violations of the Posse Comitatus Act might occur.

<u>Emergency Situations</u>

In an emergency, civilian law enforcement authority cannot waste time tracking down helicopters, dive teams, or explosive ordnance disposal (EOD) technicians. Fortunately, the military possesses a variety of capabilities to which a civilian law enforcement agency may not have access. In fact, military search and rescue helicopters and military divers frequently aid civilian law enforcement in searches for boats and missing persons on oceans, lakes, or rivers. Additionally, military EOD technicians regularly assist civilian law enforcement officials in ordnance recovery and disposal operations.

HOW TO REQUEST ASSISTANCE

There are various regulations regarding military support to civilian law enforcement agencies and the level at which DOD approval is granted varies according to the amount and duration of the support desired. For example, in many cases, base commanders can approve requests, while other requests must have higher approval. In addition, the military may require reimbursement for certain services.

The senior military law enforcement official stationed at each installation is the point of contact for these services and can provide all the necessary information regarding any rules or regulations. Law enforcement agencies near Army or Marine Corps installations should contact the Provost Marshal. Those agencies near Air Force bases should contact the Chief of Security Police, while requests for assistance from area naval bases should be directed to the Security Officer.

Every year, the U.S. military successfully supports hundreds of requests for assistance from civilian law enforcement. As stated previously, routine requests can be approved locally, and civilian law enforcement administrators should contact their military counterparts about available support. The U.S. military stands ready to provide civilian law enforcement with whatever assistance it can, in accordance with the complex stipulations of Posse Comitatus. In many cases, all an agency has to do is ask.

INTELLIGENCE OVERSIGHT

Many police administrators have no idea what "intelligence oversight" means, or how the rules that govern this law affect the way the military and the police do business. Simply put, U.S. Department of Defense organizations are prohibited from collecting and sharing certain intelligence and information on American citizens with Department of Justice agencies and visa-versa.

These laws are so restrictive that federal law enforcement agencies and military intelligence organizations are unable to share critical information regarding terrorist activity.

Because of the burden this law has placed on America's ability to fight terrorism, the United States government is presently revising some elements of this regulation.

There is much to be done by the U.S. government to address laws and regulations that are hindering law enforcement and the military from working together in the war on terrorism.

In early 2002, President Bush introduced a number measures to help the military and police combat terrorism through information and intelligence sharing, including the introduction of the U.S. Patriot Act.

America's police officers are being put in dangerous situations without the intelligence and information they need to know in order to effectively address the challenges terrorism has brought to our cites and towns.

CHAPTER 7
THE PATRIOT ACT

The Department of Justice first priority is to prevent future terrorist attacks against the U.S. mainland. Since its passage, the Patriot Act has played a key part in enabling law enforcement to protect the citizens of the United States from further deadly acts by terrorists.

The Patriot Act allows investigators to use the tools that are already available to investigate organized crime and drug trafficking.

Before the Patriot Act, courts could permit law enforcement to conduct electronic surveillance to investigate many ordinary, non-terrorism related crimes, such as drug trafficking, mail fraud, Internet crime, and organized crime. Agents also could obtain wiretaps to investigate some, but not all, of the crimes that terrorists often commit.

The Patriot Act enables investigators to gather information when looking into the full range of terrorism related crimes, including: chemical-weapons offenses, the use of weapons of mass destruction, killing Americans abroad, and terrorism financing.

The Act also allows federal agents to use high tech equipment to track sophisticated terrorists trained to evade detection.

For years, law enforcement has been using "roving wiretaps" to investigate ordinary crimes, including drug offenses and racketeering. A roving wiretap can be authorized by a federal judge to apply to a particular suspect, rather than a particular phone or communications device. Because international terrorists are sophisticated and trained to thwart surveillance by rapidly changing locations and communication devices such as cell phones, the Act authorized agents to seek court permission to use the same techniques in national security investigations to track terrorists.

One major feature of the Patriot Act is its authority to enable law enforcement officers to obtain search warrants without going through a long judicial process.

The Act gives law enforcement time to identify the criminal's associates, eliminate immediate threats to our communities, and coordinate the arrests of multiple individuals more speedily.

The Patriot Act also allows federal agents to ask a court for an order to obtain business records in national security terrorism cases. Examining business records often provides the key that investigators are looking for to solve a wide range of crimes. Investigators might seek select records from hardware stores or chemical plants to find out who bought materials to make a bomb, or bank records to see whose sending money to terrorists. Law enforcement authorities have always been able to obtain business records in criminal cases through grand jury subpoenas, and continue to do so in national security cases where appropriate.

In national security cases where use of the grand jury process was not appropriate, investigators previously had limited tools at their disposal to obtain certain business records. Under the Patriot Act, the government can now ask a federal court (the Foreign Intelligence Surveillance Court), to aid an investigation and order production of the same type of records available through grand jury subpoenas. The federal court, however, can issue these orders only after the government demonstrates the records concerned are sought for an authorized investigation to obtain foreign intelligence information not concerning a U.S. person or to protect against international terrorism or clandestine intelligence activities, provided that such investigation of a U.S. person is not conducted solely on the basis of activities protected by the First Amendment.

The Patriot Act facilitates information sharing and cooperation among government agencies so that they can better "connect the dots." The Act removed the major legal barriers that prevented the law enforcement, intelligence, and national defense communities from talking and coordinating their work with each other, to protect the American people and our national security. Now police officers, FBI agents, federal prosecutors and intelligence officials can protect our communities by "connecting the dots" to uncover terrorist plots before they are completed. Prosecutors can now share evidence obtained through grand juries with intelligence officials and intelligence information can now be shared more easily with federal prosecutors. Such sharing of information leads to concrete results. For example, a federal grand jury indicted an individual in Florida, Sami al-Arian, for allegedly being the U.S. leader of the Palestinian Islamic Jihad, one of the world's most violent terrorist groups which has been responsible for murdering more than 100 innocent people, including a young American named Alisa Flatow who was killed in a tragic bus bombing in Gaza. The Patriot Act assisted police in obtaining the indictment by enabling the full sharing of information and advice about the case among prosecutors and investigators. The Patriot Act updated the law to reflect new technologies for new threats. The Act brought the law current with new technology, so we no longer have to fight a digital-age battle with antique technology.

When investigating the murder of *Wall Street Journal* reporter Daniel Pearl, law enforcement used one of the Act's new authorities to use high-tech means to identify and locate some of the killers. Before the Patriot Act, law enforcement personnel were required to obtain a search warrant in the district where they intended to conduct a search. However, modern terrorism investigations often span a number of districts, and officers therefore had to obtain multiple warrants in multiple jurisdictions, creating unnecessary delays. The Act provides that warrants can be obtained in any district in which terrorism-related activities occurred, regardless of where they will be executed. This provision does not change the standards governing the availability of a search warrant, but streamlines the search-warrant process. The Patriot Act increases the penalties for those who commit terrorist crimes. Americans are threatened as much by the terrorist who pays for a bomb as by the one who pushes the button. That's why the Patriot Act imposed tough new penalties on those who commit and support terrorist operations, both at home and abroad.

In particular, the Act created a new offense that prohibits knowingly harboring persons who have committed or are about to commit a variety of terrorist offenses, such as: destruction of aircraft; use of nuclear, chemical, or biological weapons; use of weapons of mass destruction; bombing of government property; sabotage of nuclear facilities; and aircraft piracy.

The Act enhances the inadequate maximum penalties for various crimes likely to be committed by terrorists: including arson, destruction of energy facilities, material support to terrorists and terrorist organizations, and destruction of national-defense materials.

The Act also enhances a number of conspiracy penalties, including for arson, killings in federal facilities, attacking communications systems, material support to terrorists, sabotage of nuclear facilities, and interference with flight crewmembers. Under previous law, many terrorism statutes did not specifically prohibit engaging in conspiracies to commit the underlying offenses. In such cases, the government could only bring prosecutions under the general federal conspiracy provision, which carries a maximum penalty of only five years in prison.

In conjunction with the passage of the Patriot Act, new sharing initiatives in the war on terrorism were implemented by federal law enforcement.

The FBI expanded the terrorist threat warning system that now reaches all levels of the law enforcement and intelligence communities. Now over 18,000 state and local law enforcement agencies receive threat and warning information related to terrorist activity.

The Department of Justice established over 56 Joint Terrorism Task Forces throughout the United States, specifically tasked with investigating terrorist related activity.

Additionally, the FBI created 93 Anti-Terrorism Task Forces, one in each U.S. Attorney's district.

The Foreign Terrorist Tracking Task Force was also established by the Department of Justice, to better ensure that federal agencies, including the INS, FBI, Customs, and others coordinate their efforts to bar from the United States all aliens who are representatives, members or supporters of terrorist organizations; aliens who are suspected of engaging in terrorist activity; or aliens who provide material support to terrorist activity.

The federal government also instituted the National Security Coordination Council of the Department of Justice.

The government's success in preventing another catastrophic attack on the American homeland since September 11, 2001, would have been much more difficult, if not impossible, without the U.S. Patriot Act and the new initiatives taken by the U.S. Department of Justice.

CHAPTER 8
21ST CENTURY "GANGS"

The traditional enemies of the police and society are criminal elements who seek to destroy property and lives for personal gain. The man or woman who breaks into a house, or robs a bank, is usually looking for money to buy drugs, or for other personal reasons.

The juvenile who vandalizes someone's house, or steals a car, usually commits these acts for the "thrill." The goal of the "traditional common criminal," is to commit his or her illegal act and then get away, and avoid capture!

As we begin the 21st Century with a war in our own backyard, the police are facing an enemy unlike "traditional common criminals" who run to avoid capture after committing a criminal act.

This new brand of lawbreaker doesn't run from everyone. Instead, he or she chooses to confront anyone in their path to do one thing- kill them!

Most military and law enforcement officials agree that the best way to defeat this kind of enemy is to get to know him well. Police officers need to know everything about these new adversaries. The most important thing for the police to know is that these criminals are not like the non-violent or violent offenders they are use to confronting. Instead, these criminals are cold-blooded warriors who consider dieing as part of their mission.

Most of the violent acts committed by these criminal elements are committed in foreign nations. But as we have learned since September of 2001, America is not immune from their terror. These "gangs" are unlike the type of gangs we have ever dealt with. Police need to keep in mind that someone who belongs to one of these "gangs" may be planning to visit their town or city. Hence, it is important for the police to study the modus operandi and motives of each "gang" seeking to destroy our nation.

List of Designated Foreign Terrorist Organizations (FTOs) "Gangs"

1. Abu Nidal Organization (ANO)
2. Abu Sayyaf Group
3. Armed Islamic Group (GIA)
4. Aum Shinrikyo
5. Basque Fatherland and Liberty (ETA)
6. Gama'a al-Islamiyya (Islamic Group)
7. HAMAS (Islamic Resistance Movement)
8. Harakat ul-Mujahidin (HUM)
9. Hizballah (Party of God)
10. Islamic Movement of Uzbekistan (IMU)
11. al-Jihad (Egyptian Islamic Jihad)
12. Kahane Chai (Kach)
13. Kurdistan Workers' Party (PKK)
14. Liberation Tigers of Tamil Eelam (LTTE)
15. Mujahedin-e Khalq Organization (MEK)
16. National Liberation Army (ELN)
17. Palestinian Islamic Jihad (PIJ)

18. Palestine Liberation Front (PLF)
19. Popular Front for the Liberation of Palestine (PFLP)
20. PFLP-General Command (PFLP-GC)
21. Al-Qa'ida
22. Real IRA
23. Revolutionary Armed Forces of Colombia (FARC)
24. Revolutionary Nuclei (formerly ELA)
25. Revolutionary Organization 17 November
26. Revolutionary People's Liberation Army/Front (DHKP/C)
27. Shining Path (Sendero Luminoso, SL)
28. United Self-Defense Forces of Colombia (AUC)

Legal Criteria for Designation

- The organization must be *foreign.*
- The organization must engage in terrorist activity as defined in Section 212 (a)(3)(B) of the Immigration and Nationality Act.
- The organization's activities must threaten the security of U.S. nationals *or* the national security (national defense, foreign relations, *or* the economic interests) of the United States.

Effects of Designation

Legal

- It is unlawful for a person in the United States or subject to the jurisdiction of the United States to provide funds or other material support to a designated FTO.

- Representatives and certain members of a designated FTO, if they are aliens, can be denied visas or excluded from the United States.
- U.S. financial institutions must block funds of designated FTO's and their agents and report the blockage to the Office of Foreign Assets Control, U.S. Department of the Treasury.

Other Effects of the U.S. Patriot Act

- Deters donations or contributions to named organizations.
- Heightens public awareness and knowledge of terrorist organizations.
- Signals to other governments our concern about named organizations.
- Stigmatizes and isolates designated terrorist organizations internationally.

FTO designations expire in two years unless renewed. The law allows groups to be added at any time following a decision by the Secretary, in consultation with the Attorney General and the Secretary of the Treasury. The Secretary may also revoke designations after determining that there are grounds for doing so and notifying Congress. Additionally, the Immigration and Nationality Act defines terrorist activity to mean: any activity that is unlawful under the laws of the place where it is committed (or which, if committed in the United States, would be unlawful under the laws of the United States or any State) and which involves any of the following:

(I) The highjacking or sabotage of any conveyance (including an aircraft, vessel, or vehicle).
(II) The seizing or detaining, and threatening to kill, injure, or continue to detain, another individual in order to compel a third person (including a governmental organization) to do or abstain from doing any act as an explicit or implicit condition for the release of the individual seized or detained.
(III) A violent attack upon an internationally protected person (as defined in section 1116(b) (4) of title 18, United States Code) or upon the liberty of such a person.
(IV) An assassination.
(V) The use of any (a) Biological agent, chemical agent, or nuclear weapon or device, or (b) Explosive or firearm (other than for mere personal monetary gain), with intent to endanger, directly or indirectly, the safety of one or more individuals or to cause substantial damage to property.
(VI) A threat, attempt, or conspiracy to do any of the foregoing.

The term "engage in terrorist activity" means to commit, in an individual capacity or as a member of an organization, an act of terrorist activity or an act which the actor knows, or reasonably should know, affords material support to any individual, organization, or government in conducting a terrorist activity at any time, including any of the following acts:

(I) The preparation or planning of a terrorist activity.
(II) The gathering of information on potential targets for terrorist activity.
(III) The providing of any type of material support, including a safe house, transportation, communications, funds, false documentation or identification, weapons, explosives, or training, to any individual the actor knows or has reason to believe has committed or plans to commit a terrorist activity.
(IV) The soliciting of funds or other things of value for terrorist activity or for any terrorist organization.
(V) The solicitation of any individual for membership in a terrorist organization, terrorist government, or to engage in a terrorist activity.

There were 208 acts of international terrorism in 2003, a slight increase from 198 attacks in 2002, and a 42 percent drop from the level in 2001 of 355 attacks. (Excludes attacks on U.S. mainland).

A total of 625 persons were killed in the attacks of 2003, fewer than the 725 killed during 2002. A total of 3,646 persons were wounded in the attacks that occurred in 2003; a sharp increase from 2,013 persons wounded the year before. This increase reflects the numerous indiscriminate attacks during 2003 on "soft targets," such as places of worship, hotels, and commercial districts, intended to produce mass casualties.

Thirty-five U.S. citizens died in international terrorist attacks in 2003: Michael Rene Pouliot was killed on 21 January in Kuwait when a gunman fired at his vehicle that had halted at a stoplight.

Thomas Janis was murdered by Revolutionary Armed Forces of Colombia (FARC) terrorists on 13 February in Colombia. Mr. Janis was the pilot of a plane that crashed in the jungle. He and a Colombian service member were wounded in the crash; the terrorists shot them when they were discovered. Three U.S. citizen passengers on the plane—Keith Stansell, Marc D. Gonsalves, and Thomas R. Howes—were kidnapped by the FARC.

William Hyde was killed on 4 March in Davao, Philippines, when a bomb hidden in a backpack exploded in a crowded airline terminal. Twenty other persons died, and 149 were wounded. The Moro Islamic Liberation Front (MILF) denies any connection to the suspected bomber, who claimed he was a MILF member.

Abigail Elizabeth Litle was killed on 5 March when a suicide bomber boarded a bus in Haifa, Israel, and detonated an explosive device.

Rabbi Elnatan Eli Horowitz and his wife, Debra Ruth Horowitz, were killed on 7 March when a Palestinian gunman opened fire on them as they were eating dinner in the settlement of Kiryat Arba.

The deadliest anti-U.S. attack occurred in Riyadh, Saudi Arabia, on 12 May when suicide bombers booby-trapped cars filled with explosives drove into the Vinnell, Jadewel and Al-Hamra housing compounds, killing nine U.S. citizens. Killed at the Vinnell compound were: Obaidah Yusuf Abdullah, Todd Michael Blair, Jason Eric Bentley, James Lee Carpenter II, Herman Diaz, Alex Jackson, Quincy Lee Knox, and Clifford J. Lawson. Mohammed Atef Al Kayyaly was killed at the Al-Hamra compound. Alan Beer and Bertin Joseph Tita, also U.S. citizens, were killed on 11 June in a bus bombing near Klal Center on Jaffa Road near Jerusalem.

Howard Craig Goldstein was killed in a shooting attack near the West Bank settlement of Ofra on 20 June.

Fred Bryant, a civilian contractor, was killed on 5 August in Tikrit, Iraq, when his car ran over an improvised explosive device.

Three U.S. citizens were among the victims of a deadly truck bombing of the UN headquarters in Baghdad's Canal Hotel on 19 August. UN Special Representative Sergio Vieira de Mello was also among the 23 fatalities.

Five U.S. citizens were killed in Jerusalem on 19 August when a suicide bomber riding on a bus detonated explosives attached to his body.

They were Goldy Zarkowsky, Eli Zarkowsky, Mordechai Reinitz, Yessucher Dov Reinitz, and Tehilla Nathansen. Fifteen other persons were killed and 140 wounded in the attack.

Dr. David Applebaum and his daughter, Naava Applebaum, were killed on 9 September in a bombing at the Cafe Hillel in Jerusalem.

Three U.S. citizens were killed on 15 October in the Gaza Strip as a roadside bomb struck their U.S. Embassy Tel Aviv motorcade. They were John Branchizio, Mark T. Parson, and John Martin Linde, Jr. All three were security contractors to the U.S. Embassy.

Lt. Col. Charles H. Buehring was killed on 26 October in Baghdad during a rocket-propelled grenade attack on the Al-Rasheed Hotel. Deputy Secretary of Defense Paul D. Wolfowitz was staying at the hotel at the time of the attack.

Armed militants in Shkin, Afghanistan, killed two U.S. citizens, William Carlson and Christopher Glenn Mueller, in an ambush on 27 October. Both were U.S. Government contract workers.

From 2004 to 2005, hundreds of U.S. citizens throughout the world, including Baghdad, have been either tortured or killed by terrorists.

THE ENEMY

Al-Qaida: At War with the United States since Sept 11, 2001:

Established by Usama Bin Ladin in the late 1980's to bring together Arabs who fought in Afghanistan against the Soviet invasion. Helped finance, recruit, transport, and train Sunni Islamic extremists for the Afghan resistance. Current goal is to establish a pan-Islamic Caliphate throughout the world by working with allied Islamic extremist groups to overthrow regimes it deems "non-Islamic" and expelling Westerners and non-Muslims from Muslim countries. Issued statement under banner of "the World Islamic Front for Jihad against the Jews and Crusaders" in February 1998, saying it was the duty of all Muslims to kill US citizens—civilian or military—and their allies everywhere. Al-Qaida plotted to carry out terrorist operations against US and Israeli tourists visiting Jordan for millennial celebrations, (Jordanian authorities thwarted the planned attacks and put 28 suspects on trial), and conducted bombings in August 1998 of the US Embassies in Nairobi, Kenya, and Dar es Salaam, Tanzania, that killed at least 301 persons and injured more than 5,000 others. Al-Qaida claims to have shot down US helicopters and killed US servicemen in Somalia in 1993 and to have conducted three bombings that targeted US troops in Aden, Yemen, in December 1992. Al-Qaida is linked to the following plans that were not carried out:

- Assassination of Pope John Paul II during his visit to Manila in late 1994;
- Simultaneous bombings of the US and Israeli Embassies in Manila and other Asian capitals in late 1994;
- The midair bombing of a dozen US trans-Pacific flights in 1995;
- A plan to kill President Clinton during a visit to the Philippines in early 1995

Al-Qaida continues to train, finance, and provide logistic support to numerous other terrorist groups in support of these goals.

In 2001, Al-Qaida launched its most devastating attack on the free world in the United States, and in 2003 was responsible for bombings in Saudi Arabia, Turkey, and other parts of the world, claiming the lives of thousands of people. Al-Qaida has a worldwide reach with cells in a number of countries, and is reinforced by its ties to Sunni extremist networks.

Bin Ladin and his key lieutenants were removed from Afghanistan in 2001-2002 when the United States took the war to their doorstep. As of 2005, Al Qaida is operating in many nations, including the United States.

Abu Sayyaf Group (ASG)

Fatah Revolutionary Council; Arab Revolutionary Brigades; Black September; Revolutionary Organization of Socialist Muslims: International terrorist organization founded by Sabri al-Banna (a.k.a. Abu Nidal). This group split from the PLO in 1974 and is made up of various functional committees, including political, military, and financial. In November 2002, Abu Nidal died in Baghdad; the new leadership of the organization is unclear. First designated an FTO in October 1997 and has carried out terrorist attacks in 20 countries, killing or injuring almost 900 persons.

Targets include the United States, the United Kingdom, France, Israel, moderate Palestinians, the PLO, and various Arab countries. Major attacks included the Rome and Vienna airports in December

1985, the Neve Shalom synagogue in Istanbul, the Pan Am Flight 73 hijacking in Karachi in September 1986, and the City of Poros day-excursion ship attack in Greece in July 1988. Suspected of assassinating PLO deputy chief Abu Iyad and PLO security chief Abu Hul in Tunis in January 1991. ANO assassinated a Jordanian diplomat in Lebanon in January 1994 and has been linked to the killing of the PLO representative there. Has not staged a major attack against Western targets since the late 1980s. Relocated to Iraq in December 1998, where the group maintains a presence. Has an operational presence in Lebanon including in several Palestinian refugee camps. Authorities shut down the ANO's operations in Libya and Egypt in 1999. Has demonstrated ability to operate over wide area, including the Middle East, Asia, and Europe. Financial problems and internal disorganization have reduced the group's activities and capabilities. Has received considerable support, including safe haven, training, logistic assistance, and financial aid from Iraq, Libya, and Syria (until 1987), in addition to close support for selected operations.

<u>Al-Jihad</u>

Known as the Egyptian Islamic Jihad, Jihad Group, Islamic Jihad. Active since the late 1970s. Close partner of Bin Ladin's al-Qaida organization. Suffered setbacks as a result of numerous arrests of operatives worldwide, most recently in Lebanon and Yemen. Primary goals are to overthrow the Egyptian Government and replace it with an Islamic state and attack US and Israeli interests in Egypt and abroad. Specializes in armed attacks against high-level Egyptian Government personnel, including cabinet ministers, and in car-bombings against official US and Egyptian facilities. The original Jihad was responsible for the assassination in 1981 of Egyptian President Anwar Sadat. Claimed responsibility for the attempted assassinations of Interior Minister Hassan al-Alfi in August 1993 and Prime Minister Atef Sedky in November 1993. Has not conducted an attack inside Egypt since 1993. Responsible for Egyptian Embassy bombing in Islamabad in 1995; in 1998, planned attack against US Embassy in Albania was thwarted.

Armed Islamic Group (GIA)

An Islamic extremist group, the GIA aims to overthrow the secular Algerian regime and replace it with an Islamic state. The GIA began its violent activity in 1992 after the military government suspended legislative elections in anticipation of an overwhelming victory by the Islamic Salvation Front, the largest Islamic opposition party. First designated as an FTO in October 1997. Conducts frequent attacks against civilians and government workers. Since 1992, the GIA has conducted a terrorist campaign of civilian massacres, sometimes wiping out entire villages in its area of operation, although the group's dwindling numbers have caused a decrease in the number of attacks. Since announcing its campaign against foreigners living in Algeria in 1993, the GIA has killed more than 100 expatriate men and women—mostly

Europeans—in the country. The group uses assassinations and bombings, including car bombs, and it is known to favor kidnapping victims.

<u>Aum Supreme Truth (Aum)</u>

a.k.a. Aum Shinrikyo (Aleph): A cult established in 1987 by Shoko Asahara. The Aum aimed to take over Japan and then the world. Approved as a religious entity in 1989 under Japanese law, the group ran candidates in a Japanese parliamentary election in 1990. Over time the cult began to emphasize the imminence of the end of the world and stated that the United States would initiate Armageddon by starting World War III with Japan. The Japanese Government revoked its recognition of the Aum as a religious organization in October 1995, but in 1997, a government panel decided not to invoke the Anti-Subversive Law against the group, which would have outlawed the cult. A 1999 law gave the Japanese Government authorization to continue police surveillance of the group due to concerns that the Aum might launch future terrorist attacks. Under the leadership of Fumihiro Joyu, the Aum changed its name to Aleph in January 2000 and claimed to have rejected the violent and apocalyptic teachings of its founder. (Joyu took formal control of the organization early in 2002 and remains its leader.) On 20 March 1995, Aum members simultaneously released the chemical nerve agent sarin on several Tokyo subway trains, killing 12 persons and injuring up to 6,000. The group was responsible for other mysterious chemical accidents in Japan in 1994. Its efforts to conduct attacks using biological agents have been unsuccessful. Japanese police arrested Asahara in May 1995, and he remained on trial facing charges for 13 crimes, including 7 counts of murder at the end of 2001. Legal analysts say it will take several more years to conclude the trial. Since 1997, the cult continued to recruit new members, engage in commercial enterprise, and acquire property, although it scaled back these activities significantly in 2001 in response to public outcry. In July 2001, Russian authorities arrested a group of Russian Aum followers who had planned to set off bombs near the Imperial Palace in Tokyo as part of an operation to free Asahara from jail and then smuggle him to Russia. The Aum's current membership is estimated to be less than 1,000 persons. At the time of the Tokyo subway attack, the group claimed to have 9,000 members in Japan and as many as 40,000 worldwide.

Basque-Fatherland-and-Liberty-(ETA)

Euzkadi Ta Askatasuna: Founded in 1959 with the aim of establishing an independent homeland based on Marxist principles encompassing the Spanish Basque provinces of Vizcaya, Guipuzcoa, Alava, as well as the autonomous region of Navarra, and the southwestern French Departments of Labourd, Basse-Navarra, and Soule. Recent Spanish counter terrorism initiatives are hampering the group's operational capabilities. Spanish police arrested 125 ETA members and accomplices in 2003; French authorities arrested 46, including the group's top leadership; several other members were arrested in Latin America, Germany, and the Netherlands. In March 2003, a Spanish Supreme Court ruling banned ETA's political wing, Batasuna. Spain currently holds 572 ETA members in prison, while France holds 124. First designated in October 1997. Primarily involved in bombings and assassinations of Spanish Government officials, security and military forces, politicians, and judicial figures. During the summer of 2003, ETA targeted Spanish tourist areas. In 2003, ETA killed three persons, a similar figure to 2002's death toll of five, and wounded dozens more. The group has killed more than 850 persons and injured hundreds of others since it began lethal attacks in the early 1960s. ETA finances its activities primarily through extortion and robbery.

Al-Gama'a-al-Islamiyya Islamic Group (IG)

Egypt's largest militant group, active since the late 1970s; appears to be loosely organized. Has an external wing with supporters in several countries worldwide. The group issued a cease-fire in March 1999, but its spiritual leader, Shaykh Umar Abd al-Rahman, was sentenced to life in prison in January 1996 for his involvement in the 1993 World Trade Center bombing and incarcerated in the United States. He rescinded his support for the cease-fire in June 2000. The Gama'a has not conducted an attack inside Egypt since August 1998. A senior member signed Usama Bin Ladin's fatwa in February 1998 calling for attacks against the United States. Unofficially split in two factions; one that supports the cease-fire led by Mustafa Hamza, and one led by Rifa'i Taha Musa, calling for a return to armed operations. In early 2001, Taha Musa published a book in which he attempted to justify terrorist attacks that would cause mass casualties. Musa disappeared several months thereafter. There are conflicting reports as to his current whereabouts. In March 2002, members of the group's historic leadership in Egypt declared use of violence as misguided and renounced its future use, prompting denunciations by much of the leadership abroad. For members still dedicated to violent jihad, their primary goal is to overthrow the Egyptian Government and replace it with an Islamic state. Disaffected IG members, such as those potentially inspired by Taha Musa or Abd al-Rahman, may be interested in carrying out attacks against US and Israeli interests. Their group conducted armed attacks against Egyptian security and other government officials, Coptic Christians, and Egyptian opponents of Islamic extremism before the cease-fire. From 1993 until the cease-fire, Gama'a launched attacks on tourists in Egypt, most notably the attack in November 1997 at Luxor that killed 58 foreign tourists. They claimed responsibility for the attempt to assassinate Egyptian President Hosni Mubarak in Addis Ababa, Ethiopia in June 1995. Gama'a never has specifically attacked a US citizen or facility but has threatened US interests. At its peak they probably commanded several thousand hard-core members and a like number of sympathizers. The 1999 cease-fire and security crackdowns following the attack in Luxor in 1997 and, more recently, security efforts following September 11, probably have resulted in a substantial decrease in the group's numbers.

HAMAS (Islamic Resistance Movement)
Harakat al-Muqawamah al-Islamiyya

Hamas is the Arabic acronym for "The Islamic Resistance Movement" (Harakat al-Muqawamah al-Islamiyya). The organizational and ideological sources of Hamas can be found in the movement of the Muslim Brotherhood (MB) which was set up in the 1920s in Egypt and renewed and strengthened its activity in the 1960s and 1970s in the Arab world, mainly in Jordan and Egypt. The Muslim Brothers were also active in the Gaza Strip and the West Bank. The cornerstone of the Muslim Brotherhood is the system of essentially social activity that they call Da'wah. In the twenty years preceding the Intifada, they built an impressive social, religious, educational and cultural infrastructure, which gave them a political stronghold, both in the Gaza Strip and the West Bank. It was successful despite their lack of support for the nationalist policy of armed struggle. The Hamas movement was legally registered in Israel in 1978 by Sheikh Ahmed Yassin, the movement's spiritual leader, as an Islamic Association by the name Al-Mujamma Al Islami, which widened its base of supporters and sympathizers by religious propaganda and social work. A great part of the success of Hamas/Muslim Brotherhood is due to their influence in the Gaza Strip. The large numbers of refugees, the socio-economic hardships of the population in the refugee camps, and the relatively low status of the nationalist elements there until recently, enabled Hamas to deepen its roots among the refugees. Its emphasis on a solution that would include the liberation of all Palestine is more attractive to the Gazans, beyond the social factors that nourish the Islamic influence in that area. Another factor, which served the popularity of the Islamic phenomena, was that the Palestinian nationalist movement and the PLO moved the center of their political power away from Palestine, by consolidating an external leadership at the expense of the internal one in the Territories. In contrast, the Islamic camp and its leadership developed entirely within Palestine (al-dakhil) and could thus better serve the interests of the Palestinians. The Islamic infrastructure in the Territories was separate but parallel to the nationalist institutions built by the PLO in the 1980s. Hamas was successful in forming a social system that has provided an alternative to the social-political structure of the PLO. Hamas's prestige is based on both its ideological and practical capabilities, as a movement whose contribution to the daily life of the Palestinians is not less than its contribution to the struggle against Israel and the occupation. The significant change in the Muslim Brotherhood movement was the transition from passivity towards the Israeli rule to militancy and large-scale violent activity, especially in and from the Gaza Strip. The movement changed its name to the Islamic Resistance Movement-Hamas-and emphasized its Palestinian character and patriotism. It professed to be not just a parallel force but also an alternative to the almost absolute control of the PLO and its factions over the Palestinians in the Territories. In August 1988 Hamas published the Islamic Covenant - its ideological credo, which presented its policy on all levels of the struggle, both against Israel and the national movement of the PLO. The Hamas Covenant challenged the PLO and its claim to be the sole legitimate representative of the Palestinian people, but it did not call for its elimination. The means used by the Hamas to increase their influence in the streets were the mosques. The mosque was the first stop on the road to civil rebellion. At the same time the Hamas leaders worked at setting up the various apparatuses of the movement. In the tradition of the Muslim Brotherhood, Sheikh Yassin built the Hamas as an underground movement. He decided to separate the different apparatuses and the area activists and use only encoded messages in the internal communications. The military apparatus was called *Mujahidin*. At first, the leadership did not strive to create large numbers of activists in the organization. The aim of the founders was to set up instruments of activity that would rely on a small number of central activists. But a new generation of street leaders emerged out of the complex structural system built by the MB over the years. This generation, obedient and full of religious fervor has become the spearhead of the Islamic struggle.

At the beginning of 1991 Zaccaria Walid Akel, the head of the terrorist section of the Hamas in Gaza, set up the first squads of the Izz Al-Din Al-Qassam Battalions. In its first stages the terrorist squads kidnapped and executed people suspected of cooperation with Israel. The murder of a Kfar Darom resident, Doron Shorshan in December 1991, was the first murder of an Israeli citizen done by a Izz Al-Din Al-Qassam squads, and marked the change in Hamas's modus operandi. The basic ideology of Hamas is founded primarily on the mainstream of the Muslim Brotherhood. In the Islamic Covenant published by Hamas in August 1988, it defined itself as the "Palestinian branch of the Muslim Brotherhood". However, there is a clear distinction in the order of priorities set forth by Hamas, as opposed to those of the Muslim Brotherhood in the Territories prior to the Intifada, particularly with regard to the question of Jihad. The Muslim Brotherhood viewed Jihad as a general duty and principle and it maintained that Islam would be established first throughout the Muslim world, only later to be followed by violent Jihad against Israel, in which Palestine, too, would be liberated. Hamas stresses Jihad as the sole and immediate means to solve the problem of Palestine. Hamas defines the transition to the stage of Jihad "for the liberation of all of Palestine" as a personal religious duty incumbent upon every Muslim. At the same time, it utterly rejects any political arrangement that would entail the relinquishment of any part of Palestine, which for it is tantamount to a surrender of part of Islam. These positions are reflected in the Covenant, and in its activities. The central goal of Hamas is the establishment of an Islamic state in all of Palestine. The immediate means to achieve this goal is the escalation of the armed struggle, and ultimately all-out Jihad, with the participation not only of Palestinian Muslims but also of the entire Islamic world.

Formed in late 1987 as an outgrowth of the Palestinian branch of the Muslim Brotherhood, various HAMAS elements have used both political and violent means, including terrorism, to pursue the goal of establishing an Islamic Palestinian state in place of Israel. HAMAS's strength is concentrated in the Gaza Strip and a few areas of the West Bank. HAMAS activists, especially those in the Izz el-Din al-Qassam Brigades have conducted many attacks, including large-scale suicide bombings against Israeli civilian and military targets in late 2004.

Harakat ul-Mujahidin (HUM)

The HUM is an Islamic militant group based in Pakistan that operates primarily in Kashmir. It is politically aligned with the radical political party, Jamiat Ulema-i-Islam Fazlur Rehman faction (JUI-F).

Longtime leader of the group, Fazlur Rehman Khalil, stepped down as HUM emir, in mid-February 2000, turning the reins over to the popular Kashmiri commander and his second in command, Farooq Kashmiri. Khalil, who has been linked to Usama Bin Ladin and signed his *fatwa* in February 1998 calling for attacks on US and Western interests, assumed the position of HUM Secretary General. HUM operated terrorist training camps in eastern Afghanistan until Coalition airstrikes destroyed them in 2001.

In 2003, HUM began using the name Jamiat ul-Ansar (JUA), and Pakistan banned the successor JUA in November 2003.

HUM has conducted a number of operations against Indian troops and civilian targets in Kashmir. Linked to the Kashmiri militant group al-Faran that kidnapped five Western tourists in Kashmir in July 1995; one was killed in August 1995, and the other four reportedly were killed in December of the same year. The HUM is responsible for the hijacking of an Indian airliner on 24 December 1999, which resulted in the release of Masood Azhar, an important leader in the former Harakat ul-Ansar, imprisoned by the Indians in 1994, and Ahmed Omar Sheik, who was convicted of the abduction and murder in January-February 2002, of US journalist Daniel Pearl.

HUM has several hundred armed supporters located in Azad Kashmir, Pakistan, and India's southern Kashmir and Doda regions and in the Kashmir valley. Supporters are mostly Pakistanis and Kashmiris and also include Afghans and Arab veterans of the Afghan war. Uses light and heavy machineguns, assault rifles, mortars, explosives, and rockets. HUM lost a significant share of its membership in defections to the Jaish-i-Mohammed (JIM) in 2000. Based in Muzaffarabad, Rawalpindi, and several other towns in Pakistan, members conduct insurgent and terrorist activities primarily in Kashmir.

The HUM trained its militants in Afghanistan and Pakistan. Collects donations from Saudi Arabia, other

Gulf and Islamic states, and from Pakistanis and Kashmiris.

The HUM's financial collection methods include soliciting donations from magazine ads and pamphlets. The sources and amount of the HUM's military funding are unknown. In anticipation of assest seizures in 2001 by the Pakistani government, the HUM withdrew funds from bank accounts and invested in legal businesses, such as commodity trading, real estate, and production of consumer goods. Its fundraising in Pakistan has been constrained since the government clampdown on extremist groups and freezing of terrorist assets. The United States announced the addition of HUM to the Foreign Terrorist Organization list in 1997.

<u>Hizballah (Party of God):</u> a.k.a. Islamic Jihad, Revolutionary Justice Organization, Organization of the Oppressed on Earth, and Islamic Jihad for the Liberation of Palestine. Radical Shia group formed in Lebanon; dedicated to increasing its political power in Lebanon and opposing Israel and the Middle East peace negotiations. Strongly anti-West and anti-Israel. Closely allied with, and often directed by Iran, but may have conducted operations that were not approved by Tehran. Known or suspected to have been involved in numerous anti-US terrorist attacks, including the suicide truck bombing of the US Embassy and US Marine barracks in Beirut in October 1983 and the US Embassy annex in Beirut in September 1984. Elements of the group were responsible for the kidnapping and detention of US and other Western hostages in

Lebanon. The group also attacked the Israeli Embassy in Argentina in 1992 and is a suspect in the 1994 bombing of the Israeli cultural center in Buenos Aires. In fall 2000, it captured three Israeli soldiers in the Shabaa Farms and kidnapped an Israeli noncombatant whom it may have lured to Lebanon under false pretenses. Has established cells in Europe, Africa, South America, North America and Asia.

Islamic Movement of Uzbekistan (IMU)

Coalition of Islamic militants from Uzbekistan and other Central Asian states opposed to Uzbekistani President Islom Karimov's secular regime. Goal is the establishment of an Islamic state in Uzbekistan. The group's propaganda also includes anti-Western and anti- Israeli rhetoric. The IMU is believed to be responsible for five car bombings in Tashkent in February 1999. Took hostages on several occasions in 1999 and 2000, including four US citizens who were mountain climbing in August 2000, and four Japanese geologists and eight Kyrgyzstani soldiers in August 1999.

Japanese Red Army (JRA)

Anti-Imperialist International Brigade (AIIB): An international terrorist group formed around 1970 after breaking away from Japanese Communist League-Red Army Faction. The JRA was led by Fusako Shigenobu until her arrest in Japan in November 2000. The JRA's historical goal has been to overthrow the Japanese Government and monarchy and to help foment world revolution. After her arrest Shigenobu announced she intended to pursue her goals using a legitimate political party rather than revolutionary violence. May control or at least have ties to Anti-Imperialist International Brigade (AIIB); also may have links to Antiwar Democratic Front—an overt leftist political organization—inside Japan. Details released following Shigenobu's arrest indicate that the JRA was organizing cells in Asian cities, such as Manila and Singapore. Has history of close relations with Palestinian terrorist groups based and operating outside Japan—since its inception, primarily through Shigenobu. The current status of these connections is unknown. During the 1970s, the JRA carried out a series of attacks around the world, including the massacre in 1972 at Lod Airport in Israel, two Japanese airliner hijackings, and an attempted takeover of the US Embassy in Kuala Lumpur. In April 1988, JRA operative Yu Kikumura was arrested with explosives on the New Jersey Turnpike, apparently planning an attack to coincide with the bombing of a USO club in Naples, a suspected JRA operation that killed five, including a US servicewoman. He was convicted of the charges and is serving a lengthy prison sentence in the United States. Tsutomu Shirosaki, captured in 1996, is also jailed in the United States.

In 2000, Lebanon deported to Japan four members it arrested in 1997, but granted a fifth operative, Kozo Okamoto, political asylum.

Longtime leader Shigenobu was arrested in November 2000 and faces charges of terrorism and passport fraud.

<u>Kach and Kahane Chai</u>

Stated goal is to restore the biblical state of Israel. Kach (founded by radical Israeli-American rabbi Meir Kahane) and its offshoot Kahane Chai, which means "Kahane Lives" (founded by Meir Kahane's son Binyamin following his father's assassination in the United States.) Was declared to be a terrorist organization in March 1994 by the Israeli Cabinet under the 1948 Terrorism Law. This followed the groups' statements in support of Dr. Baruch Goldstein's attack in February 1994 on the al-Ibrahimi Mosque. Goldstein was affiliated with Kach and their verbal attacks on the Israeli Government. Palestinian gunmen killed Binyamin Kahane and his wife in a drive-by shooting on 31 December 03 in the West Bank.

<u>Kurdistan Workers' Party (PKK)</u>

Founded in 1974 as a Marxist-Leninist insurgent group primarily composed of Turkish Kurds. The group's goal has been to establish an independent Kurdish state in southeastern Turkey, where the population is predominantly Kurdish. In the early 1990s, the PKK moved beyond rural-based insurgent activities to include urban terrorism. Turkish authorities captured Chairman Abdullah Ocalan in Kenya in early 1999; the Turkish State Security Court subsequently sentenced him to death. In August 1999, Ocalan announced a "peace initiative," ordering members to refrain from violence and withdraw from Turkey and requesting dialogue with Ankara on Kurdish issues. At a PKK Congress in January 2000, members supported Ocalan's initiative and claimed the group now would use only political means to achieve its new goal, improved rights for Kurds in Turkey. Primary targets have been Turkish Government security forces in Turkey. Conducted attacks on Turkish diplomatic and commercial facilities in dozens of West European cities in 1993 and again in the spring of 1995.

In an attempt to damage Turkey's tourist industry, the PKK bombed tourist sites and hotels and kidnapped foreign tourists in the early-to-mid-1990s.

Mujahedin-e Khalq Organization (MEK or MKO)

a.k.a. The National Liberation Army of Iran (NLA, the militant wing of the MEK), the People's Mujahidin of Iran (PMOI), National Council of Resistance (NCR), Muslim Iranian Student's Society (front organization used to garner financial support). Formed in the 1960s by the college-educated children of Iranian merchants, the MEK sought to counter what it perceived as excessive Western influence in the Shah's regime. Following a philosophy that mixes Marxism and Islam, has developed into the largest and most active armed Iranian dissident group. Its history is studded with anti-Western activity, and most recently attacks on the interests of the clerical regime in Iran and abroad. Worldwide campaign against the Iranian Government stresses propaganda and occasionally uses terrorist violence. During the 1970s the MEK staged terrorist attacks inside Iran and killed several people, including

US military personnel and civilians working on defense projects in Tehran. Supported the takeover in 1979 of the US Embassy in Tehran. In April 1992 conducted attacks on Iranian embassies in 13 different countries, demonstrating the group's ability to mount large-scale operations overseas. The normal pace of anti-Iranian operations increased during "Operation Great Bahman" in February 2000, when the group claimed it launched a dozen attacks against Iran. During the remainder of the year, the MEK regularly claimed that its members were involved in mortar attacks and hit-and-run raids on Iranian military, law enforcement units, and government buildings near the Iran-Iraq border. The MEK also claimed six mortar attacks on civilian government and military buildings in Tehran.

Liberation Tigers of Tamil Eelam (LTTE)

Other known front organizations: World Tamil Association (WTA), World Tamil Movement (WTM), the Federation of Associations of Canadian Tamils (FACT), the Ellalan Force, and the Sangilian Force. Founded in 1976, the LTTE is the most powerful Tamil group in Sri Lanka and uses overt and illegal methods to raise funds, acquire weapons, and publicize its cause of establishing an independent Tamil state. The LTTE began its armed conflict with the Sri Lankan Government in 1983 and relies on a guerrilla strategy that includes the use of terrorist tactics. The Tigers have integrated a battlefield insurgent strategy with a terrorist program that targets not only key personnel in the countryside but also senior Sri Lankan political and military leaders in Colombo and other urban centers.

The Tigers are most notorious for their cadre of suicide bombers, the Black Tigers. Political assassinations and bombings are commonplace. The LTTE has refrained from targeting foreign diplomatic and commercial establishments.

National Liberation Army (ELN)—Colombia

Marxist insurgent group formed in 1965 by urban intellectuals inspired by Fidel Castro and Che Guevara. Began a dialogue with Colombian officials in 1999, following a campaign of mass kidnappings, each involving at least one US citizen, to demonstrate its strength and continuing viability and to force the Pastrana administration to negotiate.

Bogota and the ELN spent most of 2000 discussing where to establish an ELN safehaven in which to hold peace talks. The ELN is involved in kidnapping, hijacking, bombing, extortion, guerrilla war and has a modest conventional military capability. This terror group frequently assaults energy infrastructure and has inflicted major damage on pipelines and the electric distribution network.

The Palestine Islamic Jihad (PIJ)

Originated among militant Palestinians in the Gaza Strip during the 1970s. Committed to the creation of an Islamic Palestinian state and the destruction of Israel through holy war. Because of its strong support for Israel, the United States has been identified as an enemy of the PIJ, but the group has not specifically conducted attacks against US interests in the past. In July 2000, the PIJ publicly threatened to attack US interests if the US Embassy was moved from Tel Aviv to Jerusalem. Also opposes moderate Arab governments that it believes have been tainted by Western secularism. Conducted at least three attacks against Israeli interests in late 2000, including one to commemorate the anniversary of former PIJ leader Fathi Shaqaqi's murder in Malta on 26 October 1995. Conducted suicide bombings against Israeli targets in the West Bank, Gaza Strip, and Israel.

Palestine Liberation Front (PLF)

Broke away from the PFLP-GC in mid-1970s and split into a pro-PLO, pro-Syrian, and pro-Libyan faction led by Muhammad Abbas (Abu Abbas) who became a member of the PLO Executive Committee in 1984 but left it in 1991. The Abu Abbas led faction is known for aerial attacks against Israel. Abbas's group was responsible for the attack on the cruise ship Achille Lauro, in 1995, and the murder of US citizen Leon Klinghoffer.

Popular Front for the Liberation of Palestine (PFLP)

Marxist-Leninist group founded in 1967 by George Habash, a member of the PLO. Joined the Alliance of Palestinian Forces (APF) to oppose the Declaration of Principles signed in 1993 and suspended participation in the PLO. Broke away from the APF, along with the DFLP, in 1996 over ideological differences. Took part in meetings with Arafat's Fatah party and PLO representatives in 1999 to discuss national unity and the reinvigoration of the PLO but continues to oppose current negotiations with Israel.

Committed numerous international terrorist attacks during the 1970s. Since 1978 has conducted attacks against Israeli or moderate Arab targets, including killing a settler and her son in December 1996.

Popular Front for the Liberation of Palestine-General Command (PFLP-GC)

Split from the PFLP in 1968, claiming it wanted to focus more on fighting and less on politics. Violently opposed to the PLO. Led by Ahmad Jabril, a former captain in the Syrian Army. Closely tied to both Syria and Iran and carried out dozens of attacks in Europe and the Middle East during 1970s-80s. Known for cross-border terrorist attacks into Israel using unusual means, such as hot-air balloons and motorized hang gliders. Primary focus is on guerrilla operations in southern Lebanon, small-scale attacks in Israel, West Bank, and Gaza Strip.

Revolutionary Armed Forces of Colombia (FARC)

Established in 1964 as the military wing of the Colombian Communist Party. The FARC is Colombia's oldest, largest, most capable, and best-equipped Marxist insurgency. Organized along military lines and includes several urban fronts. This group engages in bombings, murder, kidnapping, extortion, hijacking, as well as guerrilla and conventional military action against Colombian political, military, and economic targets.

Revolutionary Organization 17 November

Radical leftist group established in 1975 and named for the student uprising in Greece in November 1973 that protested the military regime. This terror group is Anti-Greek, anti-US, anti-Turkey, anti-NATO, and is committed to the ouster of US bases, removal of Turkish military presence from Cyprus, and severing of Greece's ties to NATO and the European Union (EU). Initial attacks were assassinations of senior US officials and Greek public figures; added bombings in 1980s. Since 1990, FARC has expanded targets to include EU facilities and foreign firms investing in Greece.

Revolutionary People's Liberation Party/Front (DHKP/C): a.k.a. Devrimci Sol (Revolutionary Left), Dev Sol

Originally formed in 1978 as Devrimci Sol, or Dev Sol, a splinter faction of the Turkish People's Liberation Party/Front. Renamed in 1994 after factional infighting. It espouses a Marxist ideology and is virulently anti-US and anti-NATO. Finances its activities chiefly through armed robberies and extortion.

Since the late 1980s has concentrated attacks against current and retired Turkish security and military officials. Began a new campaign against foreign interests in the 1990s by assassinating two US military contractors and wounded a US Air Force officer to protest the Gulf war. Launched rockets at the US Consulate in Istanbul in 1992. Assassinated prominent Turkish businessman and two others in early 1996, its first significant terrorist act as DHKP/C. Series of safe house raids, and the arrests by Turkish police over several years has weakened the group significantly. Turkish security forces stormed prison wards controlled by the DHKP/C in December 2000, transferring militants to cell-type penitentiaries, further undermining DHKP/C cohesion.

Revolutionary People's Struggle (ELA)

Extreme leftist group that developed from opposition to the military junta that ruled Greece from 1967 to 1974. Formed in 1971, ELA is a self-described revolutionary, anti-capitalist, and anti-imperialist group that has declared its opposition to "imperialist domination, exploitation, and oppression." Strongly anti-US and seeks the removal of US military forces from Greece. Since 1974 has conducted bombings against Greek Government and economic targets as well as US military and business facilities. In 1986, the ELA stepped up attacks on Greek government and commercial interests. A raid on a safehouse in 1990 revealed a weapons cache and direct contacts with other Greek terrorist groups.

Sendero Luminoso (Shining Path, or SL)

Former university professor Abimael Guzman formed Sendero Luminoso in late 1960. His teachings created the foundation of SL's militant Maoist doctrine. In the 1980s, SL became one of the most ruthless terrorist groups in the Western Hemisphere.

Approximately 30,000 persons have died since Shining Path took up arms in 1980. Its stated goal is to destroy existing Peruvian institutions and replace them with a communist peasant revolutionary regime. It also opposes any influence by foreign governments, as well as by other Latin American guerrilla groups, especially the Tupac Amaru Revolutionary Movement (MRTA). In 2000, government authorities continued to arrest and prosecute active SL members, including, Commander Jose Arcela Chiroque.

Counterterrorist operations targeted pockets of terrorist activity in the Upper Huallaga River Valley and the Apurimac/Ene River Valley, where SL columns continued to conduct periodic attacks.

Chechnya 2004

Terrorists become more bold and violent as time goes on. In late 2004, Chechen rebels launched an attack against a Russian elementary school, killing hundreds of innocent children. The following is a news story describing what happened on that terrible day in Russia.

BESLAN, Russia—A shaken President Vladimir Putin made a rare and candid admission of Russian weakness Saturday in the face of an "all-out war" by terrorists after more than 340 people—nearly half of them children—were killed in a hostage-taking at a southern school. Putin went on national television to tell Russians they must mobilize against terrorism. He promised wide-ranging reforms to toughen security forces and purge corruption.

"We showed weakness, and weak people are beaten," he said in a speech aimed at addressing the grief, shock and anger felt by many after a string of attacks that have killed some 450 people in the past two weeks, apparently in connection with the war in Chechnya.

Shocked relatives wandered among row after row of bodies lined up in black or clear plastic body bags on the pavement at a morgue in Vladikavkaz, the capital of North Ossetia where the dead from the school standoff in the town of Beslan were taken. In some open bags lay the contorted, thin bodies of children, some monstrously charred.

In Beslan, people scoured lists of names to see if their loved ones survived the chaos of the day before, when the standoff turned violent Friday as terrorists set off explosives in the school and commandos moved in to seize the building.

U.S. Officials worry that what has happened in Russia can happen in any city across the United States. Are local cops ready for the fight?

Are America's Police Forces Ready For What May Be Coming?

Terrorist attacks in Russia
December 2002 to December 2004

- Female suicide bomber blows herself up outside Moscow's National Hotel, across from the Kremlin and Red Square, killing five bystanders. Another suicide bombing on a commuter train in southern Russia kills 44 people. Putin condemns attacks as bids to destabilize the country two days before parliamentary elections.

- Two suicide bombers drive a truck laden with explosives into a government security services building near Chechnya, killing three people and injuring 25.
- Suicide bomber rams truck filled with explosives into a military hospital near Chechnya, killing 50 people, including Russian troops wounded in Chechnya.
- Russian security agent dies in Moscow while trying to defuse a bomb a woman had tried to carry into a cafe on central Moscow's main street. Double suicide bombing at a Moscow rock concert kills the female attackers and 15 other people.
- Female suicide attacker detonates bomb near a bus carrying soldiers and civilians to a military airfield in Mozdok, a major staging point for Russian troops in Chechnya, killing at least 16 people.
- Woman blows up explosives strapped to her waist in crowd of thousands of Muslim pilgrims, killing at least 18 people in an apparent attempt on the life of Chechnya's Moscow-backed chief administrator, Akhmad Kadyrov, now the region's president.
- Suicide truck-bomb attack kills at least 60 people at a government compound in northern Chechnya. Passenger bus hits remote-controlled land mine in the Chechen capital, killing at least 8.

- Suicide truck-bomb attack destroys headquarters of Chechnya's Moscow-backed government, killing 72 people.
- More than a dozen attackers carrying guns and reportedly wrapped in suicide-bomb belts seize an elementary school in the Russian region of North Ossetia, taking hundreds of hostages, including some 200 children.
- Car blows up outside a Moscow subway stop, killing at least 10 people.
- Two airliners crash within minutes of each other after taking off from the same airport, killing a total of 90 people. Officials say explosive traces were found in the wreckage and President Vladimir Putin calls the crashes terrorist acts.
- Bomb rips through a stadium in the Chechen capital, Grozny, during a Victory Day ceremony, killing provincial President Akhmad Kadyrov, the Kremlin's point man for efforts to control separatist violence in the war-wracked region. As many as 24 people are killed. A Chechen warlord claims responsibility.
- Explosion rips through a subway car in the Moscow metro during rush hour, killing 41 people. Authorities suspect a terrorist attack.

Terrorist groups respect no boundaries. They are willing to strike anywhere on this planet and anytime of the day or night. They do not care if they kill men, women, or children.

Police officers in America must learn that the motives of these organizations are very simple; to destroy everything in their path and to kill everyone in their way. Trying to rationalize their actions is a waste of time and energy. Getting to know their leadership and how they operate is essential to developing new innovative policing methodologies in defense of our homeland.

Replace the name of any city you just read in the above catalogue of terrorist attacks in Russia, with American cities, and ask the question-Are America's police forces prepared?

In August 2005, nearly 100 British citizens in London were killed by terrorist bombings. What makes us believe such an attack cannot happen here?

(Information in this chapter was obtained from open sources on the World Wide Web).

CHAPTER 9
THERE IS A NEW KID IN TOWN

In my book 21st Century Policing, I explain that strong and innovative leadership in the police profession is very important to building successful police-public partnerships. In today's wartime environment, the same type of leadership is needed to outsmart and eventually defeat the enemies we presently face.

I also explained in 21st Century Policing, that the most difficult leadership problems law enforcement supervisors confront emanate from within law enforcement organizations, not outside of them.

Historically, police officers do not like to change from the status quo. Many cops become comfortable with the day-to-day routine. When a new leader takes over a squad, command, or an entire police department, the changes he or she institutes are usually resisted by the rank and file.

Many police officers who advance ahead of their peers and want to stay friendly with them usually fail to demonstrate effective leadership qualities. They are more concerned with their popularity among the troops rather than with the job they are required to perform.

Cops who resist change will have to learn very quickly that there is a "new kid on the block". This "kid" is not the new road sergeant, precinct commander, or police chief. The "new kid" is a terrorist. And instead of new leadership slowly changing the way cops do things, the "new kid on the block" is going to force change by attempting to kill cops and bringing destruction directly to the doorstep of police headquarters.

The first order of business police administrators must perform is to select the best and brightest people to lead America's police departments. There is no longer any room for half-hearted, politically motivated, or self serving individuals to occupy the offices which will, in a very direct way, have tremendous impact on the future of this nation.

The American people deserve the best performance possible from their law enforcement officers.

In the United States, elected politicians lead most police departments. In some law enforcement agencies a mayor appoints the top leadership as a police commissioner or police director. Civilian control over a police agency is a necessity in order to maintain checks and balances.

In the military, the civilian leader (the president) establishes policy, while military commanders run the day-to-day operations of their organizations. The chain of command in most police departments is a mirror image of the military. A civilian sets policy, while the police chief runs the day-to-day operations of the department.

Elected officials tend to exert political pressure on police chiefs in order to deliver favors for friends and supporters. When a police chief resists, he usually is pressured into succumbing to the will of the politician, or face an early retirement.

Politicians have operated in this manner for years. It is a way of life that is tolerated by all parties in the organization. For example, in 2004, Governor James McGreevy of New Jersey appointed an alleged gay lover to the critical position of New Jersey Homeland Security Director. The man the governor appointed was not qualified for the job. He was removed from his position only after a scandal broke out in 2005. This scandal also forced McGreevy to resign. When politicians like McGreevy don't take terrorism serious, disaster is sure to come.

Now that we are at war, the way politicians do business will have to change dramatically. They will have no choice but to keep their political hands off of professional law enforcement officers and limit their function to policy making. Politicians should not become involved with tactical planning and the execution of critical police operations.

Political interference in this war could result in strategic and tactical errors that could cost a number of lives. That's not to say political leadership should not be consulted and informed. There will be cases in which politicians would be required to approve specific police operations. However, politicians should know their boundaries and understand when their job ends and when the "warfighters" job begins.

Police commanders and political leaders will be required to focus on the strategic assessments which must be made and acted upon in order for their police officers to respond to emerging threats. Now is the time to gain the advantage over the enemy by assessing internal and external factors that will impact how this war is going to be fought in America's communities.

Internal factors police commanders will have to address include the way police supervisors lead their subordinates. Police supervisors will have to demonstrate intelligence, courage, character, trustworthiness, and a tempered aggressiveness if they are to be successful in this war against terrorism. Political leaders and police commanders will have to establish policies that encourage teamwork and the creation of police-public partnerships designed to increase intelligence gathering and information sharing.

External factors political leaders and police commanders will have to consider include, strategic and tactical assessments related to the infrastructure of their jurisdictions.

Questions that will have to be answered by local law enforcement agencies will include: What potential targets exist in the community? How would terrorists enter the city? By what means would they attack these targets? Once a target is attacked, by what means will the police strike at the enemy and protect the rest of the jurisdiction?

Political leaders will have to work hand-in-hand with "tactical commanders," i.e. their police chiefs and supervisory staff, in order to develop effective strategic and tactical operational plans designed to combat terrorism.

Police officers today have challenges unlike any generation of police officers in the history of this nation. To meet these challenges successfully, political leaders will have to put politics as usual aside, and police supervisors will have to "lead" in the true sense of the word. To do otherwise could mean the destruction of this great republic, block-by-block, and city-by-city.

CHAPTER 10
THE POLICE SUPERVISOR

Every young man and woman who enters a police academy graduates as a trained and disciplined professional law enforcement officer. When they see superior officers, they salute. When they speak to their supervisors they reply, “Yes sir” and “no sir.” When in uniform, they are well groomed and well dressed.

Unfortunately, soon after many new recruits leave the academy and join the rank and file of their police department, they inevitably come in contact with the “negatrons;” a group of officers who complain endlessly about their job, their bosses, and just about everything under the sun.

“Negatrons” have great impact on the efficiency of police departments. These disgruntled cops are very successful in sapping morale, causing dissension, and leading good cops into bad situations.

When the new recruit is exposed to the “club of negatrons,” the transformation from the well mannered, well groomed and well disciplined cop, to the cop who no longer salutes his superior officers and who no longer uses as part of his or her vocabulary “yes sir” or “no sir,” does not take very long.

Police leadership usually ignores and tolerates this group of unprofessional officers and allows them to “contaminate” weak willed police officers. And they eventually became charter members of the infamous "blue wall of silence club."

Once a few dozen officers are "contaminated," is doesn't take long for the entire police department to become "infected." Order, discipline, and morale breaks down and the over-all efficiency of the police department diminishes rapidly.

My military experience has taught me that there is no way any peacekeeping force or combat unit filled with "negatrons" could ever survive an engagement against an aggressive, ruthless, and disciplined enemy.

In future years, police officers in America are going to find themselves engaged in battle with such an enemy. Unless police supervisors rein in the "negatrons" that are contaminating the rank and file, the field of battle will be filled with the blood of men and women wearing blue, instead of with the blood of "criminal warriors."

Law enforcement leaders must demonstrate that they have the courage that demands action to correct problems that have the potential of breaking down the entire operation of their police department.

The chief, captain, lieutenant and sergeant, will have to use leadership skills designed to isolate the "negatrons" and to persuade officers to fulfill the vital mission of defending our nation though a shared vision.

As a police supervisor and naval officer for nearly thirty years, I have always believed that in order to gain the respect of our troops, we as leaders must constantly project characteristics which portray courage, acceptance of responsibility, self-control, knowledge, politeness, attitude of service, comradeship, modesty, self-respect and high moral standards.

Those of us in leadership positions need to understand that our subordinates view us from two sets of eyes. The first view is from the physical eye, which sees us on the job performing our sworn duty. The second view is from the "minds eye", which sees us in our personal lives at home, with the spouse, the children, or amongst the general population. I believe it is the view from the "minds eye" that has the most impact on subordinates.

If a subordinate sees his or her leader treating his family and friends with respect, the impact will be positive. If the actions of the leader are less than honorable, the impact on a subordinate could be devastating.

The character of a leader plays an important role in effective leadership. General Lemuel C. Shepherd, Jr, USMC (Ret.) once said; *"Character in my opinion is the greatest of mans virtues. It is a distinctive trait that governs an individual's patterns of behavior and is indicative of moral strength."*

Personal example is that character which conveys to each subordinate that they will be expected to do nothing that the leader has not done. If a leader is indecisive, looks shabby and projects an apathetic attitude toward the organization, the troops will lose confidence in him or her, morale will suffer, and someone may lose their life because discipline and order will break down. Leaders should convey to their troops that they (leaders) are in command! Leaders should look sharp, speak clearly, and command attention when they walk into a room.

Character is an important foundation of leadership. Without the type of character which demonstrates that a leader could take care of himself or herself, there is no way that leader will be able to convince the officers under his or her command that he or she has the ability to lead.

If you are a supervisor, or if you are going to become a supervisor in the future, prepare yourself to be a leader who will be an inspiration and role model to the men and women under your command.

From early in their career, police officers should begin the process of building the leadership foundations they will stand upon for the rest of their lives. I have always told police recruits, "Mold yourself into a shining example of a police officer that people will trust and admire".

The responsibilities of today's police supervisors are far greater than their predecessors of yesteryear. The conduct of the sergeant, lieutenant, captain and chief, off duty as well as on duty, will in some way impact on the lives of the men and women working under their command.

The leadership principles police supervisors should follow are similar to the principles many military leaders follow when leading their troops into peacekeeping or combat missions. These principles promote cohesiveness, teamwork, morale and a shared vision and determination to get the job done.

Individuals in police leadership positions must strive to educate themselves about the local and global perspectives on issues they come directly or indirectly involved with. When education ceases, the ability to lead with effectiveness stops. Good police supervisors occupy themselves with matters other then what they hear on the radio, read in newspapers, or watch on television. Good leaders need more than just "local news" as a learning tool. They need to constantly expand their horizons by gathering information and knowledge that will help them perform their duty effectively. The more knowledge a police supervisor obtains today, by studying who, what, when, where, why and how of present day issues, the better prepared he or she will be to address the issues challenging them tomorrow.

Learning is a constant for the effective police leader. Homeland defense will require learning about the modus operandi of a new enemy. Police supervisors will have to learn about the enemy's history, culture and objectives. Once this knowledge is obtained, it is the responsibility of the supervisor to share this knowledge with the men and women who will "meet the enemy on the field of battle."

Supervisors should convey to their "troops" that in this battle for our nation's survival all of them are needed. Therefore, it is up to the supervisor to develop the positive attributes of every police officer. The call to leadership is a great responsibility. SO LEAD!

CHAPTER 11
DEADLY CONSEQUENCES OF LEADERSHIP FAILURES

Every cop knows that there are supervisors in their police agencies who are apathetic, uncaring, and have negative attitudes. These supervisors make it a point to convey a message that causes the rank and file to conclude that the only reason why they (the supervisors) come to work is to collect a paycheck.

Police administrators all over the nation have tolerated such supervisors since the day policing was organized. But circumstances have now changed. No police department is going to be able to function effectively in the days ahead if they allow their leadership structure to continue malfunctioning. Many law enforcement practitioners have come to realize that by allowing supervisors who care little about their profession and the people they are called to lead, to continue functioning in today's environment, could result in deadly consequences.

Many police agencies have supervisors who fail to maintain high professional standards and fail to use the most effective management skills necessary to fulfill law enforcement's goals and objectives. During the past three decades, police professional standards have either diminished dramatically or disappeared altogether in hundreds of police agencies nationwide.

The failure of police leaders to maintain professional standards in many police agencies during the 70's and 80's resulted in low morale, bad performance, and a total breakdown in discipline and order. This failure resulted in an unprecedented growth of police corruption and unlawful acts by many police officers nationwide.

Police administrators are generally successful in identifying good and bad cops. But they fail miserably in taking the necessary action to deal with the bad cops and to commend the good cops.

In many police departments, police supervisors are more interested in being popular with their subordinates, rather than being an effective leader. And it is no secret that many supervisors turn their heads when they see a "bad cop" in action, and subsequently, do little to encourage the "good cop" to continue his or her good work.

Police department executives must be willing to challenge their personnel to maintain strong ethical, physical, psychological, and academic standards. Just about every leader in every law enforcement agency across the nation has some knowledge about officers who are truly committed to the law enforcement profession and officers who are committed only to get a paycheck.

In order to be effective, police leaders will have to identify officers whose commitment to the organization are marginal and advise them that if they fail to meet department professional standards, they will be out of a job.

Police commanders and supervisors, who fail to require officers to meet professional performance standards, add ingredients to a mixture that will result in disastrous consequences for their organizations and communities during this time of war. Hence, it is imperative that police department leaders assure that each officer is given the opportunity to sharpen his or her talents and skills by maintaining satisfactory performance standards.

In 1991, when I traveled to Israel to lecture at the Israeli National Police Academy, I learned from Israeli police commanders that their government requires every police officer to take periodic performance evaluations on topics related to law, command and control, chain of command and various policing functions. If an officer failed to obtain the minimum score in each category, he or she would be required to attend remedial training. If they failed to attain the required scores after completing this training, they would be dismissed from the police department. Israel has one of the most highly skilled police organizations in the world as a result of the rigid performance standards set by their police command authority.

Perhaps in future year's law enforcement agencies across the United States will require police officers to pass national police performance tests similar to the one Israeli police are required to complete. Such a requirement would result in preparing law enforcement agencies to meet any future challenges with the most highly skilled and trained men and women in the profession.

MANAGEMENT STYLES

Every leader has his/her own management style. The management style which works for one leader, may not work for another leader. And what may work for managing police personnel in peacetime, may not work well in a wartime environment.

Police leaders must keep their management methodologies fluid, ready to adapt to any condition resulting from a terrorist attack or terrorist related incident.

There are some management styles that will not be effective in the war on terrorism. These styles include Micro-Management, Management by Objectives (MBO), and Total Quality Management (TQM).

In peacetime and in wartime, Micro-management is the most ineffective leadership style.

In some cases, but not all, Management by Objectives runs a close second insofar as its ineffectiveness with regard to mission objectives in the war on terrorism.

Total Quality Management is a very effective methodology during peacetime, but not very effective in managing people in a wartime environment.

Since we are not at peace, law enforcement agencies will be required to take another look at these management styles and determine if any of them will be effective in formulating reactive and proactive policing methodologies.

As noted in the above paragraph, micro-management is the least effective methodology when managing people. Micro-managers lack vision and the managerial skills that are necessary to promote teamwork, good morale, discipline, order, initiative and productivity. Many micro-managers lead through intimidation and fear and therefore commit a great disservice to their subordinates. In the fight against terrorist activity, this style of management will result in mission failure. It promotes indecisiveness among the "troops" and could place people in grave danger.

Illustrations of the deadly consequences which micro-managing can have on tactical operations are found on the pages in history books that describe how American leaders fought the war in Vietnam in the 70's, and how Iraqi leaders fought the Gulf War in the 90's and the Iraqi War in 2003.

During the Vietnam War, well-trained and courageous men from the United States military were sent into combat with the goal of completing specific military objectives in order to defeat the enemy and bring the war to a close.

When the war began, military field commanders managed their troops with great success. General William Westmoreland, Commander of U.S. Forces in Vietnam, gave his field commanders the authority to make the tactical decisions necessary to win the battles they were fighting. Like every effective high-level leader, he knew that micro-management of a field commander could result in deadly consequences. So he let them do their job!

Unfortunately, Secretary of Defense Robert MacNamara did not embrace General Westmoreland's style of management. MacNamara required Washington bureaucrats to review each battle plan and approve them before a field commander could make a decision to fight.

Because of MacNamara's micro-management style of leadership, bridges that had to be bombed, enemy fortifications that had to be attacked, and enemy troops that had to be pursued were left untouched. The enemy was given time to strengthen his defenses and escape U.S. firepower because of MacNamara's micro-managing of the war.

To put this issue in perspective for the reader who is unaware of what occurred during this period of time, it is important to know that Vietcong and North Vietnamese commanders were staging their troops in neighboring Cambodia for "hit and run" missions against U.S. forces in South Vietnam.

The enemy would cross the South Vietnam-Cambodia border, attack U.S. troops, and flee back to Cambodia, a neutral nation.

U.S. field commanders developed plans to pursue the fleeing enemy across the South Vietnamese border to their safe haven in Cambodia where U.S. forces could destroy Vietcong fortifications and supply lines. To General Westmoreland's dismay, the president's Washington bureaucrats adopted a "no pursuit policy," prohibiting U.S. forces from crossing the border into Cambodia.

Although the General and his field commanders protested this micro-management of their decisions, they did not succeed in changing the president's mind. The consequences were catastrophic to U.S. forces.

Micro-managing this war was one major reason why over fifty thousand U.S. soldiers were killed and the North Vietnamese defeated the South. Nearly forty-years later, Robert MacNamara apologized to the American people for his leadership failure.

In both Iraqi wars, Saddam Hussein did not allow his field commanders to make any military decision without his personal approval. Saddam could be described as the "godfather" of micro-management. Because of his management style, U.S. and Coalition forces decimated the Iraqi military.

Some law enforcement practitioners will argue that these illustrations are not applicable to policing because they illustrate a military wartime decision-making process instead of a law enforcement mission oriented process.

I would argue that the lessons learned from using this method of managing personnel in the streets of Saigon and Baghdad can prevent a number of police commanders today from making similar mistakes when fighting the "criminal warrior" on the streets of New York, Los Angeles, and hometown USA in the years to come. Micro-management on all levels is a failed management methodology.

Total Quality Management (TQM) is a style of leadership that is essential in building trust and a shared ownership of problems and solutions the police and public face.

TQM requires supervisors to spend a good amount of time seeking input from the public and from their subordinates in efforts to find solutions to the problems plaguing our nation's cities. TQM is one of the most successful management styles leaders used in the 90's to build positive police-community relations.

However, TQM will not work in developing strategic and tactical plans that are designed to address proactive and reactive responses against terrorist activity. For one thing, police leaders will be required to maintain the utmost of confidentiality when planning responses to the intelligence and information they receive with regard to possible terrorist attacks.

Widespread public knowledge of how police departments are planning to prevent terrorist activity, or how police officers will engage terrorists on the "field of battle" could be deadly to the police. Strategic and tactical planning is for professionals, not novices who, although well intentioned, have little or no knowledge of all the facts police tactical planners will have available to them via our intelligence agencies.

Additionally, the input of field officers will be limited because the information they obtain will be fragmented. They will not have the corporate knowledge that the strategic and tactical leaders will have. Since the patrol officers knowledge of all the facts will be limited to a "local view," they will be unable to provide substantial valuable input toward developing a comprehensive and effective strategic or tactical plan designed to prevent a terrorist attack, or to engage the enemy if attacked. These officers will lack a much necessary "global view" in order to have effective input on decisions driven by unforeseen events.

Management by Objectives (MBO) is another style of management which has the potential to fail in "meeting the muster" when addressing strategy and tactics in the war on terrorism. Two major components a leader needs to employ MBO are accurate and actionable intelligence, and the ability to change objectives quickly when "battlefield" conditions rapidly change.

One problem with MBO is that once goals and objectives are set, it is near impossible to re-adjust plans when "battlefield" conditions change. When terrorists' attack, the environment becomes very fluid and conditions tend to change on a moments notice.

Micro-Management, TQM, and MBO will be of little or no value to police leaders who are fighting the war on terrorism.

We are fighting a new enemy that will require law enforcement professionals to develop new rules of engagement, and new styles of management as the global war on terrorism continues.

The next chapter introduces you to a management methodology which has the potential of being a very effective tool for police leaders to use in the war against terrorists.

CHAPTER 12
THE *L-WAID* MANAGEMENT STYLE

The *L-WAID (pronounced-L-WAYED)* style of management is designed for police leaders to meet the challenges that the war on terrorism will bring to their towns and cities.

L-WAID -Leadership With Accurate Intelligence Data is a leadership style that enables police department decision makers to lead with the best intelligence and information available for pre-operational planning and operational deployment of police officers in the war on terrorism.

It is a known fact that the side with the most accurate and current intelligence and information about his or her opponent is more likely to be the victor in any battle. Police administrators and field supervisors who establish "battle plans" from both a proactive and reactive perspective should do so only with the most accurate intelligence data available.

The *L-WAID* leadership style assures police supervisors that the decisions and plans they will be required to make is based on a "corporate knowledge" of the "criminal warriors" modus operandi as well as a progression of actionable intelligence revealing the enemy's planning and movements.

L-WAID conveys a strong message to the officers on the field that their leaders are not indecisive. This style of management eliminates confusion and uncertainty during the planning stage, and on the "battlefield."

Two of the greatest leaders this nation has given birth to are, General Robert E. Lee, Confederate Army, and General George S. Patton, United States Army. Both men lived at different times and in different places. They fought different wars and were challenged by different enemies. Both of their names went down in history as great military leaders.

Lee became known as "America's most beloved General." He put the safety and welfare of his people first. He was smart, displayed positive character to his men, was steadfast in his commitment to his nation's cause, accepted great responsibility in times of great turmoil, and joined his men on the front lines of battle.

Patton had all the qualities that Robert E. Lee had. But Patton's leadership style was quite the opposite of Lee. Known as "old blood and guts," Patton was a daredevil who met challenges head on. Anyone who tries to describe Patton's leadership skills would do him no justice. The only person, who could give us a glimpse of how Patton led, is Patton himself.

During a speech he made to a group of men he was leading into battle Patton said; *"I want you men to remember that no bastard ever won a war by dying for his country. He won it by making the other dumb bastard die for his country. I can assure you that you will do your duty. The Nazis are the enemy. Wade into them. Spill their blood. Shoot them in the belly. Now that you know how I feel, I will be proud to lead you wonderful guys into battle anytime, anywhere."*

Lee and Patton were successful in their fight against their enemies because they used the *L-WAID* style of leadership. Neither Patton nor Lee took their men into battle without first obtaining accurate intelligence to add to their corporate knowledge about the enemy. One of Patton's greatest battles was his victory over General Rommel's tanks in the desert. Patton admitted that the key to his success was the knowledge and intelligence he learned about Rommel in a book he read authored by none other than Rommel himself.

On the other hand, Lee faced his most devastating defeat at the battle of Gettysburg. For reasons still debated in classrooms across the nation, Lee led his men into combat before obtaining accurate intelligence data about the strength of the Union Army. The result of his "blunder" is now history. In both cases the intelligence and information these two leaders used or failed to use, determined the outcome of a battle.

Policing a city is not military combat. But the same leadership skills which both of these great men used could very well be used by today's police leaders who are facing great challenges.

A snapshot of how the *L-WAID* management style of leadership measures up against Micro-Management, TQM, and MBO is as follows:

<u>Hypothetical Incident & Management Styles</u>

The FBI has issued a bulletin to police departments instructing officers who respond to reports of suspicious activity near defense plants, to notify them immediately.

Police receive a report that three men are acting suspiciously in the vicinity of a defense corporation in your community. They are described as middle-eastern males in their 30s. Police are dispatched to the area of the defense plant and two patrol officers stop the subjects and begin to question them.

The leader who micro-manages goes to the scene of this incident and interrupts the on-going interview being conducted by the patrol officers. He begins to ask his own questions as to why the suspicious men are in the area. He then calls detectives to the scene and directs them to question the subjects. However, instead of letting the detectives do their job, he stays, and asks several other questions during their field interview. The supervisor never contacts the FBI, and after spending forty-five minutes investigating the subjects he is satisfied they are not a threat and tells them to leave the area, while his patrol officers are standing by scratching their heads.

Obviously, this style of leadership wastes a lot of time (forty-five minutes) and manpower, (two patrol officers, two detectives, and one supervisor). Wasting such time with regard to terrorist activity could be deadly. But this is how micro-managers work-they don't need anyone else to provide input. The micro-manager knows it all!

The supervisor who uses Total Quality Management (TQM) as a management style responds to the scene of this incident. He waits until the patrol officers' interview with the subjects is complete, and asks for an on-the-spot briefing. The officers tell him that one subject does not have identification and is insisting that the police have no right to detain him.

Instead of making a decision as to what should be done next, the supervisor asks the officers what they think should be done with the suspects. The officers tell him that they don't know. The supervisor decides to call detectives to the scene and briefs them on the findings of the patrol officers. He asks them what they think should be done. After the supervisor hears their opinion, he makes a decision to let the subjects go without contacting the FBI.

Obviously, this is not the time for a leader to conduct an opinion poll as to what to do with the suspects. It is the duty of the officer in charge to make a leadership decision one way or another.

Supervisors who fix their sights on one or two objectives use the Management By Objectives leadership style. With reference to the above-described incident, the supervisor decides that his objective is to have police officers chase the suspects away from the area.

After hearing the dispatcher send officers to the scene of this incident, the supervisor gets on his radio and instructs the patrol officers to tell the suspects that there have been complaints about them and to leave the area. The patrol officers arrive at the scene and comply with this directive. They radio the supervisor with the results. Objective achieved!

Most police officers know very well that such scenarios in many departments are not the exception, but the rule. There are many supervisors who do not want to get involved with "complex issues," and therefore look for the easy way out.

L-WAID is the management style police supervisors should use when conducting field operations during this time of war on terrorism.

The supervisor who employs *L-WAID* as his/her method of leadership begins his/her tour by reading the FBI bulletin before deploying officers out on the field.

The supervisor also directs the desk sergeant to call the FBI for further information regarding possible terrorist activity in the area. The FBI faxes a more detailed summary of suspicious activity to the supervisor.

The FBI summary includes descriptions of possible terrorist operatives, the time of day operational planning of terrorists cells usually take place, possible targets, types of surveillance, methods terrorists use to evade police, including false identification, and other vital information field officers could use in making a decision regarding suspicious individuals who are stopped and questioned.

In this case, the patrol supervisor responds to the scene of the incident after his officers arrive. He asks the officers to brief him as what they learned about the suspects. The patrol officers tell him that one of the suspects does not have identification and is evading numerous questions. Based on the intelligence information the supervisor received from the FBI at the beginning of the tour, he decides to detain the suspects and call the FBI. The FBI responds and takes custody of the subjects.

The key to the supervisor's decision to hold the suspects for the FBI was the accurate intelligence data he had in hand.

L-WAID is far more effective than any other style of leadership when dealing with this type of criminal (terrorist) activity. Had the supervisor not obtained his "corporate knowledge" from the intelligence data he received from the FBI, he may have made another decision. *L-WAID* was the driving force in his decision making process.

Obviously, this is a "snapshot" of the *L-WAID* leadership style. There are many more specifics regarding this leadership style. The major point is that by "connecting the dots" from the information and intelligence the leader obtains, results will be impressive.

CHAPTER 13
TAKING CARE OF BUSINESS

There are seven principles of leadership police supervisors will have to employ to successfully meet the challenges this war is going to bring to them.

First, be a leader! When police supervisors and managers are instructed to implement new and unpopular policies and procedures from department brass, they often distant themselves from those policies. These supervisors are more apt to say to the troops, "I just got this message from the Chief," when they should be saying, "We are going to implement a new policy."

The word "we" conveys that the supervisor *is a part of* and not *apart from*, the policies the police chief institutes. Cops conclude whether their immediate supervisor is or is not supportive of department policy by the manner in which top to bottom messages are communicated.

Police officers in leadership positions should not be in the business of trying to win a popularity contest. They should be projecting confidence in their ability to make the right decisions, at the right time, under any and all circumstances.

It is a leader's responsibility to support his or her commander whether or not he or she supports command policy. Subordinates will view leaders who convey department policies half-heartedly as weak. The job of a leader is to lead!

Second, Move forward-Not backward. Police supervisors should show their "troops" that they are forward movers and thinkers, not a backward walker or sidestepper. Many police supervisors tend to "waffle" when they are challenged to demonstrate their leadership skills under stressful conditions. They are afraid to make decisions that appear to be controversial. Not many police leaders are apt to "make waves" in the performance of their duty.

The few who are willing to "rock the boat" usually are successful in their endeavors.

A good illustration of a forward moving "boat rocker" is former NYPD Police Commissioner Bill Bratton. As Commissioner of the New York City Police Department, Bratton had many challenges to overcome. One of those challenges was to clean up Times Square.

Before Bratton took over the NYPD, former commissioners made all kinds of excuses as to why they were unable to curb the crime rate in Times Square. They pointed backwards into history citing civil rights issues, zoning laws and other reasons why they were "handcuffed" by antiquated laws, and could not clean up the area.

When Bratton took over, he moved forward by thinking ahead. He never looked back at history, he made history. The laws the former commissioners used as an excuse for their failures were used by Bratton to successfully clean up Times Square.

Third, Think "Out of the Box." As a police supervisor and Naval Officer who has great responsibilities to lead men and women, I have heard, throughout my career, many officers explain why some things can't be done. For some reason, there are always individuals who will forever find reasons why certain goals could not be achieved. These individuals lack the skills to lead and should never, ever, be placed in a command position.

In 2003, while serving in the Navy during Operation Noble Eagle, our Commanding General met with all of the officers in our command and impressed upon us that when challenged with some of the great tasks which lie ahead, we should weigh all our options before making crucial decisions. He explained that one of our options should be derived from thinking "out of the box." He told us that he wanted us to be unconventional, innovative, and risk takers. He believed that such traits gave a man or woman the right to be called a leader.

Effective leaders are willing to "go the extra mile" and put their necks out on a limb if need be. They are not afraid to make decisions. When the men and women under your command see that you are willing to walk through "the valley of the shadow of death" in order to fulfill a mission, they will gain enormous respect for you and perform well.

<u>Fourth, Take care of your people</u>. Many times patrol officers are led to believe that they are the last ones anyone cares about. Patrol officers usually get criticized in the press, in the squad room, in the commander's office, and on the street.

It is your duty to let your people know that you care about their well-being and that you will not lead them into a situation that could jeopardize their lives and careers needlessly. Let them know that you recognize them as a valuable asset to the police department and they will perform admirably.

Fifth, Be loyal. Loyalty works both ways. If you want your people to be loyal to you, you must be loyal to them. When things go wrong and you're the boss, take the heat like a real leader should. Don't let the weight of the world fall on the shoulders of your people. You will want to share the glory when they perform well, so be willing to share the pain when things go wrong.

Sixth, Get all the facts. Police departments are big rumor mills. In this new war that the police are going to be involved in, one enemy they will be challenged by is the rumor mill. It is important for police leadership to quell rumors immediately and get the facts to the troops expeditiously. Rumors will cause a breakdown in morale and performance.

Seventh, Inspire and motivate. The one thing many police supervisors fail to do is to inspire and motivate the troops. There are many ways supervisors can inspire their troops. One way to inspire them is to share with them how vitally important they are for the survival of this nation. Cops are generally good Americans. Conveying to your people that the country depends on them would not only be an inspiration, it would also motivate them.

- Be a leader.
- Move forward, not backward.

- Think "out of the box."
- Take care of your people.
- Be loyal.
- Get all the facts.
- Inspire and motivate.

These leadership principles convey a strong positive message and winning attitude to the troops in the field. Many of these principles worked for Lee, Patton, and Bratton. They could work for you!

Chapter 14
Know Your Enemy-Because He Knows You

Knowing your enemies history, strategies, tactics, skills and modus operandi is an absolute necessity in this unique war on terrorism. Without this knowledge it would be foolhardy to send any police officer into harms way. In the coming years police supervisors will have to acquire leadership skills which demand that they be well educated in the fields of history, strategy, and tactical planning.

When fighting crime, police professionals learn everything possible about how burglars, car thieves, muggers, and other "common criminals" commit their illegal acts. By obtaining this knowledge, law enforcement officers are able to develop strategies and tactics that enable them to outsmart criminal elements, thus preventing further criminal acts.

Today, police supervisors must educate themselves about America's new enemy. Once police leaders learn about who this "criminal-warrior" is, what his motives are, when and where he usually strikes, and how he intends to commit his acts of violence, they will be able to create patrol strategies and courses of action designed to prevent attacks, or respond to an attack.

The days when a patrol officer speeds to the scene of a so-called "routine incident" are long gone. In order to effectively combat terrorism in our cities, police leadership will have to create "tactical response packages" which include:

- Innovative strategic and tactical plans.
- Clearly defined goals and objectives.
- Current intelligence and information.
- Numerous approach strategies to specific incidents.
- New rules of engagement.
- Innovative exit strategies from specific incidents.

Once tactical packages are disseminated to the rank and file, the command authority of the police department will have to make sure each officer is trained and fully briefed on the elements included in them.

If this sounds like the creation of a battle plan, you are right! Supervisors will have to focus on methods designed to outwit and out maneuver a very knowledgeable and skillful enemy who has taken much time to study police department tactics, command structures, city infrastructures, intelligence capabilities, and the way police officers and other emergency services respond to critical incidents.

In fact, the enemy may have already studied how your police department operates. If you think such a statement is from "left field," you might want to think twice. Take a look at some police department Internet sites! Many police department web pages provide a lot of information to a potential enemy.

In 2003, I found a police department web page that revealed a minute-by-minute description of where patrol units were located on any given day. Such information could be a valuable tool to a well-trained terrorist cell seeking to commit a violent act in that city.

On another site, I found interesting information about a police department's explosive ordinance unit, complete with photos and a list of equipment.

And on another site, I got access to floor plans of an office building that houses a police headquarters in Virginia.

When fighting terrorists, police department leaders must keep in mind that they are fighting a warrior who will study everything about specific police departments in the cities they plan to target for attacks. This knowledge should alert you to check the Internet and find out what can be obtained about your police department and community. If what you find is troubling, it would be wise to recommend to your command authority that changes on your hometown website should be made.

Police supervisors should study the history, skills, and methods of operation, of potential terrorist organizations. This information will help police leaders to develop strategies and tactics designed to address potential terrorist activity. Department brass will need to know the enemy's goals and objectives, politics and religion, strategies, tactics, and fighting skills.

U.S. military leaders study much information about the leadership of specific enemies threatening America. As a result of the knowledge gained from these studies, military leaders are able to develop strategies and tactics designed to neutralize or defeat an enemy on the field of battle. The objective of these studies is to get into the thinking process of the enemy leadership.

With regard to the war on terrorism, our military leaders have successfully routed the enemy in the fields of Afghanistan and the cities of Iraq. It will be the job of America's police forces to rout the enemy from the streets of this nation and to prevent terrorists from turning our neighborhoods into battlefields.

Police officers should be as aggressive in learning about terrorist organizations as they have been to learn about organized criminal syndicates and the drug cartel. By learning about the leadership of the mob and drug organizations worldwide, the police have been successful in hindering their ability to do business in America. The mob is slowly becoming a footnote in the history books of the future, and the drug cartel is soon to follow.

Do you have enough knowledge about terrorist organizations threatening America? Can you develop strategic and tactical plans to prevent terrorists from successfully striking at your community? These are questions that are haunting police leaders nationwide.

Terrorist groups first select a target. Then they launch an information-gathering operation to learn about the specifics of their selected target. The information they seek includes the target history, security measures to defend the target, construction material of the target, and other information that would enable them to execute a successful attack. During the planning stage, terrorist groups learn how the police and other emergency services respond to emergencies. They will know how many police officers they will have to engage in "combat" if necessary; from what direction police will be coming; and other vital information critical to their operation.

Terrorists usually plan to destroy a primary and secondary target. The primary target is usually a fixed structure and the secondary target is usually the police, fire fighters, and other emergency units responding to the scene of the initial attack.

The Israeli police have learned that during the planning stage, a terrorist operative would call the police and report that a bomb is located in a specific building, ready to detonate. Other operatives would fan out near roadways leading to the intended target observing everything going on between the time the call to the police is made and the time the police respond to and arrive at the scene of the incident. Terrorists note their observations and plan their attack accordingly.

The common criminal who plans a bank robbery would make similar observations before launching his operation. However, his reason for wanting to know the specifics of a police response is to plan a timely escape. The reason why terrorists gather all this information has nothing to do with trying to plan a fast getaway. Terrorists want this information to do one thing, kill the police responding to the scene of the incident.

In foreign countries, terrorists have been known to place bombs directly in the path of emergency vehicles, and detonate them at precisely the moment these vehicles are on top of them. Remember, their goal is not to escape the police-it is to kill the police.

Police leaders will be able to outwit terrorists by including in their strategic and tactical planning packages counter-terrorism plans designed to thwart pre-operational planning methodologies terrorists use prior to an attack.

Chapter 15
Changing Priorities
-Strategic & Tactical Planning-

In my book 21st Century Policing, I advocated quality of life and proactive community policing methodologies as the means to combat crime at its roots. For community policing to be effective, police departments have to gain and maintain public support over a very long period of time. Community policing has to be the top priority of every police department in America for the police to effectively reduce crime and improve police-community relations. The objective of community oriented policing is to make life so miserable for potential criminal elements; they would move to the next city and hopefully find no safe haven for their ill-gotten trade.

The strategic goals of proactive community policing are to reduce crime, foster positive police-community relations, and to improve citizens' quality of life. In many cities and towns throughout the United States these strategic goals were achieved in the late 90's.

The tactical plans to achieve the goals of community oriented policing are designed to transform the cop who was once "*apart from*" the community, to the cop who is "*a part of*" the community. Crime has been reduced in major cities and the image of the police has changed from predominately negative to positive, as a result of community policing.

I never thought I would ever be saying that community policing could no longer be law enforcement's priority. As a strong advocate of community policing methodologies for over 20 years, I worked with a generation of police officers who labored very hard in bringing the people and the police together during law enforcement's most difficult times. However, circumstances in America have changed. Community-policing methodologies alone will not be enough to combat terrorist activity.

Terrorists with new weapons, means that the police must create new strategic goals, tactics, and priorities to combat this enemy. Indeed, community policing should continue. But as long as we are at war, policing priorities must shift from building police-community partnerships designed to improve police-public relations, to encourage the creation of police-public partnerships for the purpose of designing and executing strategic and tactical plans that strengthen specific police operations and intelligence capabilities to combat terrorism.

In order to achieve such a dramatic transformation, we are going to have to educate America's law enforcement officers and the general public about new policing priorities and objectives.

Strategic goals will have to focus on preventing terrorist attacks in our cities and the methods police will use to destroy the enemy if he strikes. Preventing most terrorist attacks in our cities is a goal that is attainable. However, the destruction of the enemy is much more difficult to achieve.

In order to defeat the "criminal warrior," police department rules of engagement and use of force policies will have to change dramatically.

Traditionally, police departments needed only to view the world within the borders of their community when designing strategic goals and tactical plans to fight crime. However, from top management to the patrol officer on the street, the way police do business will have to change if we are to succeed in our fight against terrorists.

The priorities of America's police departments in the 20th Century were focused on strategic plans designed to prevent crime through various proactive policing methodologies and on tactics designed to quickly apprehend criminals who committed crimes within specific jurisdictional borders. As a result of the war on terrorism, police supervisors will no longer have the luxury of supervising or managing from the seat of a patrol car, or office. They will have to get involved in the "fight" by getting out of the car and out from behind the desk. Supervisors will have to work with the "troops" on the field and interact with their colleagues who work in bordering cities and towns. What goes on in neighboring communities is no longer to be ignored. It will be important for police departments to share information and develop strategic and tactical policing plans that include mutual aid, intelligence sharing, and other types of assistance if needed.

Police administrators will have to develop policing methodologies that will reflect stronger police action when confronted with a terrorist act.

It is important for police officers and their leaders to know the strategic goals and tactical methods of the terrorist cells they are dealing with. Terrorists want to dismantle the United States Government by attacking its civilian population and infrastructure. Their strategy was revealed by the attacks on the World Trade Center in NYC, which represented America's economic structure, and the Pentagon, which represented America's military might. And if the third aircraft was enroute to the Washington D.C. before it crashed in Pennsylvania, a sacred symbol of America's government would have been destroyed.

The tactical methods of terrorists are designed to spread fear by bombing buildings and killing innocent people. In future year's terrorists most likely will attempt to spread chemical and biological weapons against civilian targets.

Obtaining as much knowledge as possible about this ruthless "criminal warrior" could mean a matter of life and death, not just for a cop, but also for an entire city.

Although the U.S. military has brought the war to the enemy's homeland, we must not forget that the enemy has brought this war to our neighborhoods.

Police department strategic goals must be focused on dismantling terrorist cells by using non-traditional tactical methods in both reactive and proactive phases of policing. Some non-traditional tactical policing methods could include: Creating a military-police partnership with regional military reserve intelligence units and police units; Re-assigning detectives who normally investigate "traditional criminal activity" such as narcotics, burglaries and other non-violent crimes against persons and property, to anti-terrorist investigations; Re-training and re-configuring SWAT Teams and police tactical units to include urban warfare and military type tactical combat methods, in the event their service becomes necessary.

Police-community programs like DARE, school resource officers, and other programs which take cops off the street will have to be revisited and in some cases eliminated in order to keep as many police officers as possible, on the streets.

These dramatic changes will not sit well with the cops who enjoy these jobs. But they must realize that national security is a top-priority that requires everyone to sacrifice something. The changes in the way police do business will not sit well with the enemy either. More cops on the streets could very well mean the less number of terrorist operatives roaming our neighborhoods.

Business as usual in every police department in America is coming to a slow but sure end. I am not advocating that we abandon or neglect the crime problems that routinely plague our cities and towns. But our priorities must change from addressing "routine" police work to addressing extraordinary circumstances and situations that will arise during this extraordinary time in our history.

CHAPTER 16
REVOLUTION IN POLICE AFFAIRS TEAMS

The first order of business for America's police executives in this new century should be to begin "thinking out of the box." That is, to think in terms about formulating non-traditional, revolutionary policing methodologies designed to meet the challenges terrorists are bringing to our nation.

By nature, individuals who maintain leadership positions in police departments are inherently conservative. Many of these leaders do not think in terms of the future because they are use to a very comfortable past. But as a result of the potential terrorist threats that are lurking at the doorstep of every city and town in America, police leaders will be forced to re-think the way they do business.

A recent report published by the United States Commission on National Security outlined some of the new threats and challenges our nation will be facing in this new century.

The commission specifically stated that the United States will become increasingly vulnerable to hostile attacks on the homeland and that these attacks will come in the form of non-traditional means through acts designed to terrorize civilian populations.

In 1993, the United States got a taste of this non-traditional nature of warfare when terrorists attacked the World Trade Center in New York City, and failed to destroy one of the two Twin Towers.

Japan got a taste of this non-traditional warfare in 1995, when terrorists spread the nerve gas Sarin in a Tokyo subway.

In September 2001, the United States was plunged into a global war after terrorists completed their 1993 mission by totally destroying the World Trade Center Twin Towers in New York City, killing over 2,000 civilians; by attacking the Pentagon in Virginia, killing hundreds of military and civilian personnel, and by causing the crash of an airliner they skyjacked to attack another target, killing all the passengers.

In order for the police to be prepared for potential terrorist activity in their communities, law enforcement leadership should consider developing Revolution in Police Affairs Teams (RIPATs).

It would be advantageous for police agencies to create Revolution In Police Affairs Teams (RIPATs) comprised of law enforcement professionals tasked with creating innovative ideas and technologies designed to transform the way in which police do business.

There will be much opposition to the "think-tanks" which the RIPAT will be creating as their leaders grapple with the threats our nation is facing. Change is something police bureaucrats don't accept easily. But leaders who support the RIPAT concept must stay the course and work hard to overcome any opposition they encounter. There is too much at stake to ignore new ideas and concepts that could result in saving our nation from great harm.

Machiavelli's *The Prince* describes the difficulties that come along with change. He once said, "*One should bear in mind that there is nothing more difficult to execute, nor more dangerous to administer than to introduce a new system of things; for he who introduces it has all those who profit from the old system as his enemies, and he has only luke warm allies in all those who might profit from the new system.*"

In the late 1990s, when policing was evolving from being reactive to proactive via community relations programs, police nationwide resisted. It took nearly 10 years to fully implement community policing as an acceptable practice for fighting crime in thousands of cities and towns across America.

The heart of the problem regarding "change" is leadership. Many leaders in the police profession are too comfortable in their "ivory tower." They are part of an institutional cancer that hinders progress by refusing to allow fresh innovative ideas to flourish.

In past years "ivory tower" leaders were tolerated or ignored. They are the "dead weight," which must be removed from the job. As a nation, we can no longer afford to tolerate their poor leadership; nor can we afford to spend time, manpower and money listening to their endless arguments about why police departments should not change "successful" policies.

Police leaders nationwide must accept change or be forced to leave office. And the public must acknowledge the need to change policing tactics, or be forced into a kind of change that will be delivered to their neighborhoods by terrorists.

The bottom line is very clear. If we fail to change the way police do business in this nation, we risk the danger of being dissected by a crafty and ruthless enemy, block-by-block and city-by-city.

The way to introduce change is to start a "revolution" in thinking, strategy, and tactics. Such a "revolution" will make policing our communities in the future much smarter than it is today.

CHAPTER 17
"WARTIME" POLICING METHODOLOGIES I
-INTELLIGENCE GATHERING-

With America at war, policing methodologies are going to have to change dramatically in order to keep the population and infrastructure safe from the enemies of our nation. The first order of business will be for the police and the people to work together in partnership like never before in American history.

In the late 90s, when community policing was the trend of police departments nationwide, the police and the people forged partnerships to address quality of life issues that helped reduce the crime rate. Now, with these community partnerships in place, police agencies can use their relationship with the people as a foundation for what must become their number one policing priority-intelligence gathering.

Historically, there has been no common thread to identify policing priorities and methodologies across the United States. The number one policing priority of every police department differs across the nation. In New York, the priority the police may be addressing is organized crime. In Chicago, it may be narcotics. In some communities, priorities may range from burglaries, to petty thefts. America's police departments must now weave a common thread across the nation that identifies one common policing priority-the defense of the homeland through information and intelligence sharing.

Gathering intelligence on organized crime members is nothing new for police departments. At the very least, most police agencies have some know-how on intelligence collection requirements when investigating organized crime or drug cartel members.

However, there is a vast difference between gathering intelligence on organized crime, drug cartel groups and suspected terrorist cells. Investigators will have to be trained in new ways to deal with new threats.

Contrary to what some law enforcement practitioners believe, gathering intelligence on terrorists is not that complicated. In fact, it might be easier (in some instances) to gather intelligence about suspected terrorist activity than organized crime members.

Police departments across the United States can collect vital intelligence and information on suspected terrorists by utilizing their partnerships with the people who live and work in the neighborhoods they patrol.

There are three basic steps police departments can implement for intelligence and information gathering of possible terrorist activity.

First, the Chief of Police should create a Police Department Homeland Security Intelligence Bureau (HLSIB). The purpose of this bureau is to collect, analyze, disseminate and take action on any information that may directly or indirectly appear to be linked to possible terrorist activity. Police officers assigned to Homeland Security Intelligence Bureaus can be trained by national law enforcement or military police experts, through numerous government-training programs, including military assistance to civil authorities (MACA).

Second, once the HLSIB is established, two supervisors should manage the bureau. One supervisor will manage incoming and outgoing intelligence and information. He will reach out to the citizens who are members of "Neighborhood Watch," and provide them with guidelines they can use to keep an eye out for suspected terrorist activity. He can also manage the information the public provides the police and manage the flow of information to and from other law enforcement agencies.

The other supervisor will be the "action officer." His job will be to make sure action is taken on all terrorist related information flowing into the police department. He will track investigations, make sure all leads are followed-up, and work closely with the Federal Bureau of Investigation and other federal law enforcement agencies.

Third, a system to fuse information provided by the public into the HLSIB should be established. Information from the public could be forwarded to the Homeland Security Intelligence Bureau via police reports, Internet, phone calls, or write-in.

The Importance of Intelligence & Information

One month after the September 11th 2001, attack on New York City, an elderly women living in a northern New Jersey community reported to her local police department that she observed "something unusual" about her Middle Eastern looking neighbor. When police investigated, they found that the "something unusual" was something bigger than what they would have ever expected. The following is what the police report revealed.

"On October 15th, 2001 Mrs. XXXXX of XXXX, New Jersey, stated that at approximately 0730 she was walking down the hallway of her apartment when her neighbor, (in apartment 000) opened his door and exited. As she said hello to him, she glanced inside his apartment and noticed that there was no furniture. What caught her attention was a map of the United States on a wall with red marks on it. She stated she would not normally think anything of such a matter except for the fact that her neighbor is of Middle-Eastern decent and the Attorney General was on television the night before asking citizens to report anything they deem to be suspicious."

No crime was committed. Hence, before September 11th, the police would have probably ignored such a report and the woman would have probably ignored what she observed.

However, in the wake of the attacks of September 11th, this citizen was aware enough to observe the map on her neighbor's wall, which she believed was exactly the type of information the Attorney General wanted reported.

Police detectives assigned to interview the woman learned that the "suspicious man" was from Pakistan who owned a telecommunications company in NJ. For approximately four months prior to September, he had numerous visitors of Middle Eastern decent at his apartment and on a few occasions he questioned people in the area about police patrols and neighborhood watch.

Police also learned that he owned companies in three southeastern states and was depositing over $25,000 in cash every week in a local bank. A background check on him revealed information that required the attention of the FBI and INS. Federal authorities continued the investigation and the suspect was subsequently detained. It was learned that he could have been connected to terrorist activity.

From the report of one citizen who took the Attorney General's request to report any suspicious activity seriously, the police found themselves unfolding what appeared to be a link to terrorism.

The police department, now realizing how valuable their citizens could be in intelligence gathering, established a Homeland Security Bureau.

This incident portrays the importance of intelligence gathering as the number one priority of policing in today's wartime environment. What will never be known is what possible terrorist act was prevented and how many lives were saved as a result of one solitary alert citizen.

Unfortunately, not all police departments are taking such calls seriously. In February of 2005, a police officer from a northern NJ community received a call from a woman who lives in another northern NJ community, telling him that she observed suspicious activity in her neighborhood. She described what the officer believed had the "fingerprints" of potential terrorist activity. The officer advised her to contact her local police department, adding that he was sure they would conduct an investigation.

The next day she called him back and told him that her local police thought she was nuts and that no action was taken. The officer was prudent enough to direct her to the FBI. It ended up that this "nut" came up with some interesting information that may have been related to terrorism.

CHAPTER 18
"WARTIME" POLICING METHODOLOGIES II
-NETWORKING-

Most police departments lack the manpower and money to establish individual intelligence units in their police agencies. Police administrators who are in charge of manpower allocations usually assign a number of their officers to duel roles, spreading their workload as much as possible.

To overcome what may seem to be overwhelming obstacles prohibiting some police departments from establishing new policing priorities designed to meet today's challenges, police departments can assist each other by organizing Homeland Threat Working Groups, comprised of detectives from various police jurisdictions who would network with each other by sharing intelligence and information about specific threats that may impact their individual jurisdictions.

Detectives who specialize in computer crimes, finances and surveillance techniques, should be included in this working group. By sharing these resources, time, money, and manpower would be used more effectively and valuable information would be available for each police department participating in the working group.

The HTWG concept is a good way to provide detectives with a fundamental knowledge of the terrorist cells that may be operating in their area of responsibility. Anti-terrorism experts from the FBI and other law enforcement organizations can provide valuable information about these groups.

As I have said throughout this book, knowing your enemy is vital to addressing potential terrorist activity. When detectives are investigating possible terrorists' operatives, they should know about their training techniques, methods of operation, history and leadership.

This knowledge will help investigators develop unique investigation techniques that will reap valuable information about potential terrorist activity in their community.

Conducting investigations of possible terrorist links to suspicious activity is similar to investigating other criminal activity with one exception. Local police investigators are going to have to rely heavily on federal law enforcement authorities that have the expertise in dealing with the "criminal warrior."

Too often police agencies adopt the "protect our own turf" attitude and refuse to allow other law enforcement agencies to "interfere" with their investigations. The idea behind such a position is that when the "big guy" is captured, the local police department and no one else will get the credit. Likewise, some "feds" play the same game.

In this war, there is no room for egotistical leaders who play games. When local police find a suspected terrorist or terrorist link, they should know enough to call the people who are trained anti-terrorism experts. To do otherwise can result in disastrous consequences.

Also, federal authorities should routinely notify local police about terrorist activities that may affect their community.

As of this writing, search and seizure laws, detention laws, and other laws regarding what police can do in the course of an investigation insofar as terrorism is concerned, are being revised. It is imperative that investigators review and learn about the most recent guidelines established by the Attorney General's office before they begin investigating suspected terrorist activity.

Police-Public Networking

Networking information between the police and the public is as important as police sharing information with each other. Police-public networking and information sharing can be achieved through a number of ways.

Crime watch, neighborhood watch, police-citizen partnerships and other police-community programs have successful track records in combating crime.

The key to successful networking with the people who live and work in our communities is for the police department to keep the police-public lines of communication open twenty-four hours a day, seven days a week, and 365 days a year.

Once the public is convinced that their local police department is very serious about receiving public input with reference to suspicious activity possibly linked to terrorist activity in their neighborhoods, the wealth of information the police receive may play a major part in preventing an attack.

Police officers will have to learn what to look for, what questions to ask, what answers to give, and what information to release to the public. The public will have to learn what to look for, how to communicate what they observe as "possible terrorist activity," and what not to do when participating as the extended eyes and ears of the police. State and federal anti-terrorism task forces could help local police agencies train and educate the public about their role in this effort.

Police officers generally like to do all the talking when responding to certain incidents. Now they must get use to do a lot of listening and demonstrate a high level of patience when people are giving them information related to the war on terrorism. No small amount of information is insignificant when addressing terrorism issues. Officers must allow everyone offering them information about anything they believe may have a connection to terrorist activity to speak without hindrance.

It is unfortunate that many police officers feel that the public is bothersome at times, or that some information people bring to them is petty. Fortunately, most cops on the street are pretty good with the people, and work with them no matter how "petty" a matter may seem to be.

However, police-public problems usually surface with desk officers and dispatchers who are insensitive to public needs. Desk officers and dispatchers can make or break public confidence in a police department by the way they treat a citizen. In this wartime environment, if a dispatcher sends the wrong signal to the public as a result of a negative attitude, the consequences could be deadly.

All the officers in the police department need to understand how important it is to be patient and understanding of someone who offers information they believe to be vital in the war we are engaged in.

Police are going to have to "go the extra mile" to help the public understand that any information they (the public) believe has a terrorist link should be reported. The police will have to convey to the people that if what they report is not linked to terrorist activity, they should not be discouraged from reporting future observations. It is better to report what one might believe to be terrorist related and find out later it is not, than not report a suspicious incident for fear that it will turn out to be nothing, and find out later it was something significant. There is no "petty reporting" in a wartime environment.

Don't Worry About It-Go Home

A lesson from the failure to network, share, and report critical information was learned the hard way in the early morning hours of December 7, 1941, when two army officers working at a radar station on the Hawaiian Islands spotted hundreds of "blips" on their radar screen.

When they called the watch officer to report what they believed to be very unusual activity on the radar screen, the watch officer told them not to worry. He explained that the blips were probably a squadron of American warplanes returning from a drill. The soldiers replied by telling the watch officer that he might want to check this matter out a little further and make some calls to see if the "blips" were in fact, American planes. The watch officer told the soldiers, "don't worry about it, go home." Twenty-minutes later, nearly one thousand military personnel and civilians were killed by hundreds of Japanese warplanes, and America entered World War II.

As the soldiers who saw the "blips" on their radar screen, citizens today may see "blips" on their "radar screen" when they observe something unusual. It would be prudent for the police not to tell the citizen, "Don't worry about it-go home."

CHAPTER 19
"WARTIME" POLICING METHODOLOGIES III
-PATROL METHODOLOGIES-

Police department patrol methodologies in every city and town across America are different. Some police agencies use directed patrol, others use reactive patrol, and others rely on foot and bicycle patrol methodologies as a primary means to combat specific criminal activity.

Patrol officers are America's most important assets in the war on crime. And in the coming years, they will be the greatest assets in the war on terrorism. What police officers see and hear during their days and nights of patrolling is going to be of critical importance in preventing terrorist attacks.

Historically, police agencies have shied away from assigning patrol officers to the same patrol zone each day they report for duty. The reason for this is that many years ago big city police officers who patrolled neighborhoods where organized crime took root, were paid off by mobsters to "look the other way" when crime syndicates started to conduct business.

In the 1970s, the motion picture "Seprico" revealed how dozens of New York City Police Officers assigned to the same patrol zones each day took payoffs from mobsters who were selling drugs, shaking down businesses and committing other criminal acts.

One cop, Frank Seprico, refused to take payoffs and was nearly killed by a fellow officer who was on the mob payroll. He survived, and his testimony in a court of law led to the arrest and conviction of dozens of police officers in the biggest corruption scandal in American police history.

Today we are fighting a war which will require police administrators to reconsider a return to assigning "the same cop to the same beat" in order to provide the police department with maximum intelligence and information. Cops who patrol the same neighborhoods day in and day out learn everything about every person who lives and works in their patrol zone. They know who is married, who is divorced, who is working, who is out of work, who has a cold and whose kid is graduating from high school. The most effective means to combat terrorist activity in any community is to obtain credible intelligence. The most effective method to get the most credible intelligence is to deploy police officers to permanent patrol zones.

After September 11th 2001, a New Jersey police department that assigned patrol officers to six month rotations in the same patrol sector learned from one of the officers that during a four-month period in 1999, he noticed a number of people in two cars parked in an empty lot across the street from a defense plant during lunchtime, taking photos of the plant.

What aroused the officer's suspicion was that the people in the cars were not from the neighborhood. They were all dark complexion males with beards. The neighborhood was predominantly Irish. He knew the neighborhood residents well. The officer wrote down license plate numbers in his logbook in the event a crime was later discovered in the neighborhood.

After six months, a new officer rotated into this patrol zone. On his first week of patrolling near the defense plant, he noticed some men taking pictures of the plant from the empty parking lot. But not knowing the neighborhood demographics, he didn't think anything of it. He had no reason to take plate numbers or question why they were in the neighborhood. They were not doing anything illegal. So he went about his business.

After September 11th, 2001, it dawned upon the officer who, in 1999, took the plate numbers from the cars of the suspicious men taking pictures of the defense plant, that they could have been surveilling the plant as a possible target. He reported his observations, now nearly two years later, to his superior officers.

Police administrators immediately asked every officer who rotated into that zone if they observed any picture taking between 1999 and 2001. All the officers assigned to that patrol zone stated that they saw people taking pictures of the plant from time to time but didn't bother to inquire.

If the first officer had been permanently assigned to this neighborhood, he would have no doubt obtained more information about the suspects. This information may have led toward a link to terrorist activity. We will never know!

By moving this officer from one zone to another, vital intelligence and information at a critical period in time was lost. Of course, if September 11th did not happen we would not be discussing this topic. But it did happen and as I said in a previous chapter, times have changed! Extraordinary events will mean changing policing methodologies during these extraordinary times.

We can argue the fact that the officers rotating in and out of the zone should have shared the intelligence and information they individually obtained. But as many in the police profession know, cops are reluctant to share anything. Perhaps they will now.

CHAPTER 20
JOINT WARFIGHTING

America is at war! Our leaders are going to have to revolutionize the way the military and police forces in our nation do business. Law Enforcement leaders are going to have to develop a joint war-fighting concept that integrates police and military forces, especially in the area of information warfare and homeland security.

The kind of policing that was unthinkable before September 11, 2001 is now a necessity if we, as a nation, expect any chance of total victory over terrorism in the years to come. The battlefield is no longer isolated in a foreign land. The fight for freedom has come to our nation and on the enemy's terms. Not since the 1700's have we had to fight for freedom in our own back yard.

There are numerous challenges that must be addressed in order for the joint war-fighter to effectively combat the enemy. Some of these challenges deal with the merging of civil and military authorities. Other challenges deal with antiquated intelligence oversight laws that are hindering our homeland defense capabilities.

One challenge we can begin addressing today is that of building a joint war-fighting capability for homeland security by using America's reserve military forces and local police forces in partnership, to fight this war.

This new concept of a joint war-fighting force would have the primary mission of achieving victory through proactive joint war-fighting methodologies, rather than through reactive means.

In this war, a reactive response by our forces against an enemy who has launched a homicide attack that kills many Americans is a victory for him and a defeat for us. Hence, our focus must be on proactive policing methodologies.

The United States Armed Forces has always had the necessary land, sea, and air power to confront and defeat an enemy anywhere on this planet with the exception of one place-the United States of America. We are a nation that has always been prepared to bring the fight to the enemy, on his turf and on our terms. But now the enemy has brought the fight to our turf, and on his terms. The tactics our enemies use against us will require a change in our strategic thinking and tactical planning.

During the past five decades the best military war-fighting planners in America developed strategies and tactics designed to defeat former super-power and other cold war enemies who threatened us with nuclear war. When the super-power (Soviet Union) and her allies fell, our military strategists and tactical planners had to shift gears and develop plans to fight and defeat third world enemies in the jungle or on desert terrain.

As a result of the September 11, 2001 attacks, war-fighting planners who designed strategies and tactics for cold war and third world country battlefields will now have to develop plans which will move the fight from the jungle and desert onto a new battlefield, the streets of cities like New York, Chicago, and Washington D.C.

In past years when most people heard the term "war-fighting," they would recall television and newspaper images of troops in the field of battle with guns blazing, tanks rolling, ships sailing and aircraft flying into a war-torn area of battle in a far off land. People would recall images of battles that took place in lands such as the Philippines, Europe, Korea, Vietnam, and Iraq.

Prior to America's "new day of infamy" people would recall images of coastal, air, and land warfare far from the shores of this nation when the topic of war-fighting was discussed at home, in school, or in the workplace.

Today, old images of warfare have been replaced by new images of tall buildings ablaze, and by the blood of innocent men, women, and children being spilled, not in a country far from our shores, but on the streets of our own cities.

We must learn from the September 11th attacks that the Navy, Army, Marine Corps, Air Force, Coast Guard and National Guard, will not in their individual capacity project enough power on earth to defeat this new warrior who has invaded our land.

Without new and innovative joint war-fighting strategies and tactics that include all branches of the military in partnership with local civil authorities, victory will elude us.

Military commanders tasked with the defense of the homeland will have to reshape U.S. military forces to meet the challenges of this new kind of warfare in our newest area of operations, (AOR) North America.

Leaders in command authority will have to begin planning new strategic and tactical warfare scenarios that require the utilization of "joint war-fighters" on two fields of battle. One field of battle is where the "intelligence war" on a computer screen against the enemy is on-going. The other field of battle is where the deployment of a "joint battle force," here and overseas, by either police or military forces in reaction to hostile acts, is taking place. Both forces must maintain combat readiness at all times.

The forces on the "silent battlefield," where intelligence is being collected and analyzed by military and civilian authorities, is essential for the war-fighters in the fields and on the streets to be effective and victorious against the enemy.

In reshaping our forces and by creating new strategic and tactical scenarios for homeland defense, military command authorities will have to include in the joint war-fighters "mix" the front line "war-fighter," the police officer.

It is clearly understood that police officers are not expected to fight a trained warrior armed with powerful weapons. However, in this joint war-fighting environment, police officers can harness America's most important weapon in this war; information and intelligence. And they can provide suppression of pre-operational planning by terrorists groups through various policing methodologies.

By being our best and most effective human intelligence resource, the police officer who patrols his or her neighborhood can have profound impact on our combat readiness insofar as homeland security is concerned.

The intelligence and information a "street cop" can provide federal and military authorities could close gaps, connect links, and enable law enforcement and military organizations to better plan the deployment of combat air patrols, coastal patrols, border patrols, and street patrols. Valuable time, money, and manpower could be saved with the inclusion of the local police as *a part of*, instead of *apart from*, the "joint war-fighting" matrix.

Experience in war fighting has taught us that air power alone cannot defeat an enemy. Ground forces are an absolute necessity for decisive victory. And before ground forces can enter the fight, accurate and actionable intelligence must be obtained.

It will take a joint war-fighting force comprised of the best intelligence analysts in the military and police forces to win this war. We will need to develop a joint war-fighting force which is capable of outsmarting and outwitting the enemy through the fusion of military and law enforcement intelligence and information which, after being processed, will be communicated to the "battlefield commanders" (military and police leadership).

Police will use this information to develop proactive tactical plans designed to find the enemy and suppress his plans before he is able to fire one shot. Where proactive measures are inadequate, this intelligence and information would enable the military battlefield commander to assist local police by either deploying his forces to meet and defeat the enemy, or by implementing military operations other than war (MOOTW).

In order to sustain an effective level of combat readiness for homeland defense through a total joint force that includes both military and civil authority, military command authorities and police administrators will be required to assess the pool of expertise and talent which now exists in every military reserve component and police department in the nation.

Harnessing "untapped" knowledge and "unused" talent for the purpose of collecting, analyzing, and disseminating valuable and useable intelligence and information for use by both military and civil authorities will help in the development of an effective joint war-fighting capability.

Military reservists from all branches of the armed forces and police officers from all over America represent a cross section of our society. The knowledge and talent they have is immeasurable. The contacts they have in government and in thousands of small communities and large cities are invaluable toward a "total war-fighting capability."

As active military forces project power forward and maintain a high level of combat readiness in other

AORs (areas of responsibility) worldwide, military reserve units in partnership with civil law enforcement can effectively maintain an equally high level of "combat readiness" and project forward power in American cities without negatively impacting combat readiness elsewhere.

The way to achieve this unique joint war-fighting capability is to create new Joint Force Command Homeland Security Reserve Units, across the nation. These units can be newly established elements as part of a DOD and homeland security partnership, or they can be established as components of presently assigned military reserve units in each state.

These joint force units would be comprised of men and women from Army, Navy, Marine Corps, Air Force, Coast Guard, National Guard intelligence units and federal, state and local police liaisons. They would have the primary responsibility for collecting, analyzing, and disseminating intelligence packages which include threat assessments, threat patterns, and courses of action (COA's) for specific areas identified as vulnerable to a terrorist attack. These intelligence packages would enable the military and police to effectively determine practical, realistic, and prioritized layers of protection against threats to their assets and infrastructure.

Joint Force Units would monitor on-going developments affecting specific AORs and fuse military intelligence and law enforcement information into a "one stop, all source" threat assessment package which would provide the framework for both police and military organizations to work together in the development of pre and post incident response plans.

This concept of war fighting and policing will raise eyebrows. But it is a concept that is designed to draw all our resources together in the fight against a ruthless enemy.

Every police department in the United States of America can play a vital role in the war on terrorism. One of the first actions police administrators should take is to schedule anti-terrorism and counter-terrorism training for their officers. This training should include, but not be limited to:

- Urban warfare tactics;
- Communication skills;
- Proactive anti-terrorism patrol methodologies;
- Intelligence and information gathering techniques;
- Study of the Posse Comitatus Act and Intelligence Oversight Laws;
- Study and review of federal, state, and local laws regarding the detention of suspected terrorists.

Training sessions can be held at regional police academies and instructors can be contacted through state and federal law enforcement agencies. A police officer's knowledge of the above subjects would make him or her more effective in addressing issues related to terrorism.

Police administrators should begin organizing Homeland Threat Working Groups to network and share intelligence and information with numerous police departments in their region.

Networking with other police agencies by organizing Homeland Threat Working Groups is a method that will enable police departments and other law enforcement agencies to share vital intelligence and information about possible terrorist activity in each jurisdiction.

ORGAINIZING A HOMELAND THREAT WORKING GROUP (HTWG)

- A police supervisor and patrol officer should be assigned as members of the HTWG. It will be their job to exchange information about terrorist activity with other law enforcement agencies.
- The supervisor and patrol officer can organize and host an HTWG in your area by selecting a topic for the invited group of officers to discuss. A guest speaker who has knowledge about anti-terrorism topics should be invited. Speakers could be found by contacting organizations such as the:
- FBI;
- CIA;
- INS;
- Office of Naval Intelligence;

- Office of Special Investigations, U.S. Army;
- Naval Criminal Investigative Service;
- Air Force Office of Special Investigations;
- Office of Homeland Security;
- Book Authors and Commentators;

Once a speaker is scheduled, each police agency in the area should be notified and invited to send a representative to attend. It would be advantageous for the host police department to establish a HTWG membership roster by using FEMA regions as a guide; or by establishing its own regions.

Once the host police department receives replies, an agenda can be transmitted or mailed to the invited departments. Meetings can be held monthly or quarterly. The HTWG can create a newsletter for its members.

CHAPTER 21
PROACTIVE WARFARE

Since the re-emergence of community policing two decades ago, police departments throughout America have used proactive patrol methodologies in the fight against crime. Proactive patrol is designed to "stop crime before it happens," through police visibility and public participation in crime prevention programs.

Now that we are at war, proactive policing methodologies should be enhanced to include strategies and tactics designed to prevent and deter potential terrorist acts.

As discussed in previous chapters, public observations and reports of suspicious activity are part of the proactive policing methodology that has a very successful track record in preventing crime. Police should encourage citizens to continue their efforts in keeping the crime rate down and to include reports of observations that they believe to be terrorist related.

The police can be extremely proactive in identifying possible terrorist targets in their community. With this information they can tailor patrol functions and implement other measures to protect potential targets and suppress a potential enemy.

For example, if your community has a large company with a fuel tank farm on it, that tank farm could be a potential target for terrorists. Hence, it would be prudent for the police department, in partnership with the Office of Emergency Management, to visit the site of this company and conduct a vulnerability assessment of the tank farm. The vulnerability assessment would include:

- Type and construction of target;
- General location;
- Specific location;
- Possible methods of attack;
- Layers of protection against attack;
- Courses of action emergency services would take in the event of an attack.

After the vulnerability assessment is complete, the police department would tailor patrol and other emergency functions to protect the target as best possible from an attack.

EXAMPLE OF VULNERABILTY ASSESSMENT

Type and construction of target: Fuel Tank Farm, made of iron.
General location: 125 Main Street, Anytown, USA
Specific location: Fuel tanks are in the middle of the company compound. One tank is 100 yards from a river used by small boats; a four-lane highway borders three other tanks.
Layers of protection against attack: Two unarmed guards are posted at the complex entrance.

Possible methods of attack: A car loaded with explosives on site; air attack by using a small plane; use a small boat and shoulder harnessed missile to attack from the river.

Courses of action recommended by police and emergency services:

- Replace unarmed guards with trained armed guards.
- Erect concrete barriers at entrance to prevent a speeding car from entering compound.
- Assign marine police or company security to patrol river.
- Assign frequent police patrols on the highway bordering the complex.
- Educate employees about the modus operandi of terrorists.
- Request FAA restrict light aircraft from flying over complex.

Vulnerability assessments find the weaknesses of a potential target. Put yourself in the enemy's shoes and plan a hypothetical attack against the weaknesses you find in your community. Then develop a course of action to prevent the attack.

In 2002, while meeting with an army general during my tour as a naval officer in Operation Noble Eagle, I remarked to him, *"Everyday which goes by without America suffering from the result of a successful terrorist attack is a day of victory for us and a day of defeat for them."* I am convinced that proactive policing can play a major role in defeating the plans of an enemy seeking to destroy targets all over this nation.

Police administrators should continuously update terrorism watch lists they receive from the FBI and other federal law enforcement agencies. Watch lists should be disseminated to all police officers on the department and to the public when necessary. Watch lists could be disseminated a number of ways:

- Posted on poles;
- To residents via neighborhood watch captains;
- Local cable television stations;
- To the public at large via local business establishments.

Police officers patrolling neighborhoods should develop police-public partnerships designed to enhance public participation in the war on terror. Partnerships should include, but not be limited to enhanced neighborhood watch programs which include training Neighborhood Watch Captains:

- On what to observe and what to report as possible links to terrorist activity;
- On profiling of criminals/terrorists;
- On what kinds of potential targets terrorists look for;

- On what methods of operation terrorists use to find targets.
- On organizing quarterly Situational Awareness Meetings (SAMS) enabling the police and public to:
    - Exchange ideas about how to protect the community;
    - Address rumors;
    - Discuss public concerns.

Police departments can partner with veterans groups to encourage businesses and homeowners to fly American flags all over the community. If there is any message that demoralizes the enemy it is the one communicated by flying Old Glory on every street, in every city in America. This may seem like a minor thing, but in a war of this type, it is not!

Police officials and the public can also support changes in laws that are designed to strengthen law enforcements ability to protect their communities against terrorist attacks. People need to get involved by voicing their support for the police and military by writing letters and voicing their support at public meetings, or in the media. Information warfare involves everyone, including the people who live and work in America's cities.

Not since the American Revolution has America been at such a crossroads. For over 200 years the U.S. government kept the military and civil police at a distance by staying away from forming a national police force similar to police forces in foreign lands.

Because of circumstances beyond the control of the American people, the distance between the military and police must close, especially in the areas of intelligence gathering, information sharing, and tactical responses to terrorist acts.

People opposed to "nationalizing" anything related to police will rise in fury against suggestions like creating a national data bank on suspected terrorists, or the fusing of military and civil law enforcement data, or permitting police to detain people who are deemed national security risks.

Posse Comitatus and Intelligence Oversight laws should reflect some restrictions that would prohibit too much government intrusion on the people. But in time of war, some of these restrictions should be lifted for the good of the nation.

The process that allows an unprecedented partnership between civilian police agencies and the U.S. military must begin today. We cannot afford to wait for tomorrow.

And we must work hard to get the people and local police directly involved in the war on terrorism through unique partnerships designed to share vital intelligence and information.

Many unwise bureaucrats in positions of leadership have created policies, strategies, and tactics by viewing the world from "inside the box." It is time to support leadership willing to view the world from "outside the box." These are the leaders who will help bring about the dramatic positive change needed to revolutionize the way the police and the military do business in the years to come.

On September 11, 2001, the sun set on an innocent fun loving United States of America. On September 12th 2001, the sun, in its bright splendor awakened over a land determined to give her military organizations and police forces the instruments of war and the tools of peace they need to keep this great nation as the land of the free and the home of the brave.

AUTHORS NOTE: Much information in this book was obtained from open sources on the world-wide web. Where an author, commentator, or writer of such information was known, credit was given. Information related to terrorists groups was obtained from a list published by the U.S. State Dept, on the WWW.

For additional information on how you can establish proactive policing programs in your community contact www.AmeriCop.org, or email AmeriCopUSA@aol.com or write, AmeriCop PO Box 225, Nutley NJ 07110.

(Most of the information provided in chapter 6 & 7 was provided through open source documents, briefs, and commentaries on the World Wide Web).

Paperback Books from AmeriCop are Available from WWW.IUNIVERSE.COM

- Cops & God
- Soldiers & God
- Sailors & God
- Marines & GOD

Pocket Prayer Partners for Police and Military are available from AmeriCop at no cost. Just write: AmeriCop, PO Box 225, Nutley NJ 07110; call toll free 1-866-263-7267; or email: AmericopUSA@aol.com. Also request a copy of our free newsletter-*Cornelius*.